Cover Illustration/Publication Design: Yancy Young
Art Production: Ralph Fowler
Typesetting: Carol Iversen
Photo: Howard Kaish


Printed in the United States of America
First Printing November 1979
Second Printing January 1980

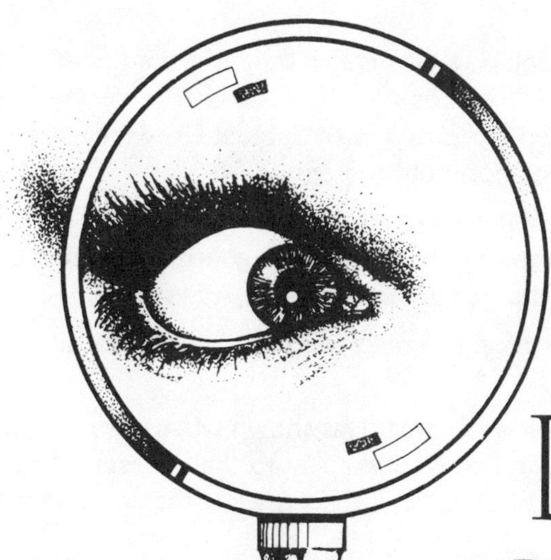

# The GOURMET DETECTIVES...

***Reveal the Secret Recipes of Famous Southern California Restaurants***

Harriet Part ◦ Sherry Watnick

# Introduction

Harriet Part shown on the left of her "*Cooking Cousin*" . . . . Sherry Watnick, is a University trained Home Economist. Upon her graduation from U.C.L.A. she was featured in the Food section of the Los Angeles Examiner under her own by-line, Prudence Penny, Jr. After several years as a columnist, she accepted a position with Sunkist Growers where she was in charge of their recipe section as well as being responsible for their food photography.

Sherry Watnick was born and raised in the French Provinces of Canada, where girls learn to poach fish instead of playing with dolls. After marriage brought her to the United States she continued her interest in gourmet cooking by studying under several noted American teachers, notably Rita Leinwand, the Food Editor of Bon Appetit.

Brought together by their common interest in the culinary arts, these two young women founded the Les Cousines Cuisinieres Cooking School, a success from its very beginning.

Throughout the dozen years of their operation the girls noted that the greatest interest was shown when they offered a series featuring restaurant recipes. Those in the classes took a special joy in being able to say to their guests, "*This is like the Apple Tart from Le Restaurant*". Now, the authors, through their book, afford their readers the opportunity to bring to their own tables a bit of their favorite restaurants.

How many times has a prospective buyer picked up a book of restaurant recipes to find that a chef has neglected to include his famous Gateau St. Honore, substituting instead his not so famous, "*Apple Pie with a slice of American cheese*."

Great restaurants are built around great chefs, and great chefs are not about to give away their stock in trade to anyone with the price of a cookbook.

Enter *The Gourmet Detectives,* two enterprising women who teach at their own cooking school, Les Cousines Cuisinieres; and have developed their versions of these most wanted restaurant recipes.

Also included in the book are other class favorites that help to create perfect party menus for entertaining at home.

*The Gourmet Detectives* is just what the name implies, a gastronomic adventure, by the authors, into the secret world of restaurant recipes.

Harriet Part · Sherry Watnick

# Contents

We gratefully acknowledge the use of the following Restaurant Recipes . . . some given willingly, some hinted at and some spied upon.

# A Far East Adventure

TRADER VIC'S CHI CHI

TRADER VIC'S CRAB RANGOON

GRAND STAR'S TOMATO BEEF CHOW MEIN

DRAGON PALACE'S MOO SHU PORK

FLAMING PEACHES

## TRADER VIC'S CRAB RANGOON

1 lb. pkg won ton skins
1/2 lb. crab meat
1/2 lb. cream cheese
1/2 tsp. A-1 Sauce
1/4 tsp. garlic salt
Sesame seeds
Whole egg or water

Combine crab meat, cheese, A-1 sauce, garlic salt and sesame seeds. Have whole beaten egg ready, damp towel, plastic wrap and a small spoon. Keep skins covered with damp towel. Fill won ton skins by putting a teaspoon of filling in center of each wrapping. Fold to the center. Gently press edges together. Fold in half lengthwise; then fold back and bring ends together. Dab a little egg or water on one corner, put 2 corners, one over the other and press together. Put filled won tons side by side on trays and cover with plastic wrap. Fry in deep fat heated to 360' for 1 to 2 minutes or until golden brown. Drain. Keep warm in 200' oven until all are cooked, then serve. Or, cool, package and freeze. To serve, arrange while still frozen on cookie sheets. Bake in 350' oven for 10 to 15 minutes or till crisp. Makes approximately 5 dozen.

## FLAMING PEACHES

8 Elberta Freestone peach halves
1/2 cup butter
1 1/2 cups brown sugar
1/2 cup heavy cream
2 Tbsp. brandy
Vanilla ice cream scoops
1 tsp. freshly grated nutmeg

Melt butter in chafing dish. When it bubbles, add peaches cut side down. Add brown sugar. Stir carefully around the peaches until sugar is dissolved. Turn peaches over and over. Add nutmeg. Continue basting allowing sauce to bubble but not to burn. Add cream. It might curdle, but blend with stirring.

Heat brandy in little pan. Ignite and pour flaming into chafing dish. Blend. Pour sauce over peach half served with vanilla ice cream. Makes 6 - 8 servings.

*Flaming Peaches was a recipe originated by Fred Waring's mother and featured many years ago at the Villa Fontana by Robert Balzer who was the food manager at the time.*

## GRAND STAR'S TOMATO BEEF CHOW MEIN

1/2 lb. fresh or dry noodles
2 Tbsp. oil for frying noodles
1/2 lb. beef (flank or sirloin), sliced thin
1 Tbsp. cornstarch for beef
5 Tbsp. oil
2 tsp. curry powder or more to taste
1 cup green pepper pieces
1 cup onion, cut into pieces
3 Tbsp. soy sauce
1 tsp. salt
1 Tbsp. cornstarch for tomatoes
1/2 cup water or stock
4 medium tomatoes, peeled and cut into wedges
2 tsp. sugar
1 Tbsp. tomato paste

Boil fresh noodles in salted water for 3 to 4 minutes. (Cook dry noodles according to package directions). Drain and run cold water through. Spread noodles in frying pan with 2 Tbsp. oil to fry until golden brown on each side. Put noodles on platter and keep warm in oven.

Mix sliced beef with cornstarch and 1 Tbsp. of oil. Over low temperature, heat remaining oil in wok. Fry curry powder for 1 minute. Add green pepper, onion, soy sauce and salt to pan. Turn up heat and stir fry for about 2 minutes. Remove to bowl. Add beef to wok and stir for 2 more minutes. Add to bowl. Stir cornstarch and water until smooth. Add tomatoes to wok along with sugar and tomato paste and cook slightly. Stir in cornstarch mixture, cook and stir and then add beef and vegetables. Stir a few more minutes and put on top of noodles. Makes 6 - 8 servings.

## TRADER VIC'S CHI-CHI'S

Fill blender a little more than half-full with crushed ice. Put in 3 pineapple slices or spears. Add pineapple juice to fill. Add 2 tablespoons Hawaiian Snow, 3 jiggers Vodka. Add more crushed ice if needed. Blend for a few seconds. Serve with cherry and spear of pineapple. Makes 3 to 4 servings.

*Because it's so perfect for entertaining, one of our students made up "batches" of Chi-Chi's ahead of time. Her husband, who taste-tested as they went along, never made it to the party! Beware, its delicious, but lethal.*

## DRAGON PALACE'S MOO SHU PORK WITH MANDARIN PANCAKES

*Moo Shu Pork:*

2 pork steaks, cut into thin strips
1 tsp. salt
1 Tbsp. + 1 tsp. cornstarch
1 bunch green onions, sliced thin
2 sml. carrots, cut into thin slivers
1/2 cup bamboo shoots, slivered

2 eggs, lightly beaten
1 1/2 Tbsp. soy sauce
2 Tbsp. Sherry
1/2 cup chicken broth
1 tsp. sugar
Hoi Sin Sauce

In a wok, heat about 3 Tbsp. oil, add pork, which has been mixed with cornstarch and salt. Fry until pink disappears. Drain into bowl. Add more oil if necessary to wok; heat. Add green onions, carrots, and bamboo shoots. Stir for a few minutes, drain and add to pork. Add egg mixture and cook stirring until partially set. Remove to bowl. Combine soy sauce, Sherry, chicken broth and sugar. Mix cornstarch with a little water. Return meat, vegetables, and eggs to wok; add soy mixture and blend in cornstarch. Mix till heated through.

## MANDARIN PANCAKES
### (Continued)

*Pancakes:*

2 cups flour
1 cup boiling water
Sesame oil

Put flour into bowl. Add water in a stream, stirring until mixture forms a warm dough. Turn out on floured board and knead for 2 minutes. Cover and let stand for 15 minutes. Shape dough into a cylinder 2 inches in diameter. Cut the roll into 1 inch slices. With hee! of hand, flatten to 3 inch rounds. Brush tops with sesame oil. Sandwich two rounds together, oiled surfaces touching. Roll out on floured board (roll from center out) to about 6 inches in diameter. Sandwich and roll out remaining dough. Heat a griddle over moderate heat and cook each pancake until it starts to bubble, turn it over and continue to cook until browned. Separate pancakes as they are cooked and stack on plate and keep covered with dampened cloth. Can be made ahead, refrigerated, and later reheated by steaming or reheating in 300' oven for 10 minutes.

*To assemble:*

Place steamed pancake flat on a plate. Brush with Hoi Sin Sauce in center of pancake. Put about 2 Tbsp. of filling on top of sauce. Roll pancake, folding one end to prevent dripping.

*Judge Kathleen Parker recommended this restaurant to us and we've been faithful followers ever since.*

# You'll Be An "Eastern Star"

TWIN DRAGON'S HOT SOUR SOUP

SHANGHAI WINTER GARDEN'S SHRIMP IMPERIAL

MANDARIN WOK'S SPICY CHICKEN WITH PEANUTS

POLO LOUNGE'S COCONUT MOUSSE

## TWIN DRAGON'S HOT SOUR SOUP

3 Tbsp. cornstarch
1/3 cup water
1/4 cup soy sauce
1/4 cup wine vinegar
1/2 tsp. white pepper
1 oz. bean curd, optional
1 extra large egg, beaten
2 dried Chinese mushrooms, soaked and drained
1/2 sml. chicken breast, cooked and cut into thin slivers
1 Tbsp. oil
1/4 cup sliced green onions
1 inch piece ginger, peeled, grated
4 cups chicken stock
1/2 tsp. salt
1 tsp. sesame oil
6 - 8 chopped small shrimps, cooked

Blend the cornstarch with the water. Add the soy sauce, vinegar, and pepper. Cut bean curd into 1/4 inch squares. Beat egg with a fork. Cut mushrooms and chicken into thin long pieces.

Heat oil in large saucepan. Add green onions and ginger and stir for a minute. Add mushrooms, shrimp, and chicken and stir for another minute. Add the stock and bring to a boil. Turn heat to moderate. Stir in cornstarch mixture until soup thickens. Add bean curd and continue to simmer. As you stir soup with a fork, slowly pour in beaten egg so that it separates into threads. Add salt and sesame oil. Serve hot. Makes 8 - 10 servings.

*We talked to the chef; he told us everything we wanted to know; we just didn't understand a word he said. Our taste buds did the work for us.*

## SHANGHAI WINTER GARDEN'S SHRIMP IMPERIAL

1 lb. medium shrimp, shelled and cleaned
Salt
Oil
2 cloves garlic, pressed
1 Tbsp. grated fresh ginger
2 - 4 small red chile peppers, crushed
3 green onions, sliced

2 Tbsp. soy sauce
2 Tbsp. chicken stock
1 Tbsp. dry Sherry
1 Tbsp. vinegar
1 Tbsp. ketchup
2 tsp. sugar
Dash Sesame oil

Pat shrimp dry with paper towl. Sprinkle shrimp with salt. Cover wok lightly with oil and heat until oil is hot. Quickly saute shrimp over high flame until shrimp turns white. Add all other ingredients except the onions and sesame oil. Cook, stirring until shrimp are coated and most of the liquid has evaporated. Add onions and cook a few seconds longer. Serve immediately. Makes 4 - 6 servings.

*After three separate dinners and thirty glasses of water, we finally captured "the aroma of the wok."*

## MANDARIN WOK'S SPICY CHICKEN WITH PEANUTS

3 lge. chicken breasts,
  boned and skinned
2 Tbsp. cornstarch
1 egg white
Salt
1 cup skinned peanuts
1 Tbsp. cornstarch

2 Tbsp. water
4 scallions, chopped in ½" pcs.
2 tsp. sugar
1 1/2 Tbsp. vinegar
2 Tbsp. soy sauce
1 1/2 Tbsp. oyster sauce
3-4 tsp. coarsely chopped dried red chiles

Partially freeze chicken and then dice. Mix chicken with cornstarch, egg white and salt. Chop peanuts coarsely. Combine cornstarch and water; set aside. Combine sugar with vinegar, soy sauce and oyster sauce and chiles in small bowl.

Put 2 - 3 Tbsp. oil in wok. Heat until oil browns a piece of scallion. Add chicken all at once but then quickly separate pieces and stir-fry. Remove with slotted spoon to bowl. Add peanuts to wok and stir for a few seconds. Remove to bowl with chicken. Add scallions, cook a few seconds and remove to same bowl. Drain fat from wok. Add sugar and liquid mixture to wok and cook for 20 seconds. Add cornstarch mixture just enough to thicken slightly. Return chicken mixture to wok and stir and cook until heated through. Makes 4 - 6 servings.

## POLO LOUNGE'S COCONUT MOUSSE WITH STRAWBERRY SAUCE

2 cups half & half
3 envelopes unflavored gelatin
1/3 cup water
1 cup sugar
1 tsp. coconut flavoring
3 cups heavy cream
4 Tbsp. powdered sugar
1 Tbsp. Amaretto liqueur
2 cups flaked coconut

In a saucepan heat half and half to boiling point over moderate heat. Soften gelatin in water for 5 minutes and stir into boiling cream along with sugar. Turn heat to very low and stir until gelatin and sugar are dissolved. Pour into bowl and cool in refrigerator until mixture is thick and syrupy. Fold in coconut and flavoring. Whip cream, adding liquer and powdered sugar. Fold into coconut mixture. Spoon mousse into oiled 8-cup mold. Chill until firm. Makes 10 - 12 servings.

*Strawberry Sauce:*

Partially defrost 2 boxes frozen strawberries and with steel blade of food processor, run through for few seconds. Pass in separate bowl.

*The Polo Lounge refused to divulge this recipe. Twenty-seven dollars and a month after the case was opened, The Gourmet Detectives had the recipe. Now one of our students says her husband comes home for lunch whenever she makes this dessert.*

# Oh! Mama Mia

TORTA RUSTICA

VALENTINO'S ROLLATINI OF CHICKEN

VALENTINO'S RIGATONI AL FORMAGGI

NEW YORK CHOCOLATE CHEESECAKE

# TORTA RUSTICA

1 pkg. (13 1/4 oz.) yeast hot roll mix
Sausage and Tomato Filling
2 Tbsp. beaten egg

Prepare hot roll mix as directed on the package. After the dough has risen, turn onto lightly floured board and knead to expel air bubbles, for about two minutes. Divide dough in half. Roll one portion on floured board into 10-inch round. Fit dough into bottom of a greased 10-inch spring form pan. Cover evenly with filling. Roll remaining dough into a 9-inch square and cut strips about one inch wide. Place the strips over the filling in crisscross fashion, tucking ends of dough down around filling at pan rim. Lighly cover dough and set in warm place for 30 to 40 minutes. Uncover and brush top with beaten egg. Bake on lowest rack of 350′ oven for 35 to 40 minutes. Cool for 5 minutes, then remove pan rim.

*Sausage and Tomato filling:*

1 1/2 lbs. Italian sweet sausage
1/2 cup finely chopped parsley
4 Tbsp. Parmesan cheese
1 cup well drained canned sliced baby tomatoes (or use sliced fresh plum tomatoes)
Salt and pepper to taste
Pinch of oregano
2 cups shredded Mozzarella cheese

Remove sausage from casing. Saute meat until pink disappears, stirring; remove from heat and pour off fat. Add parsley and Parmesan cheese. Spread filling on dough, top with tomato slices, season to taste with salt and pepper and oregano, then sprinkle Mozzarella cheese over.

## VALENTINO'S ROLLATINI OF CHICKEN

4 large whole chicken breasts, boned and skinned
2 chicken thighs, boned and skinned
1 clove garlic
2 oz. mushrooms, cut into pieces
1 cup torn fresh spinach
1 Tbsp. chopped parsley
3/4 cup white wine
1 Tbsp. Sherry
1/2 tsp. salt, dash pepper
1 egg
Flour
Oil
1 small onion, chopped
1 stalk celery, chopped
1 small carrot, chopped
Pinch rosemary
3 Tbsp. butter
1/2 (6 oz.) can tomato paste
Salt and pepper

Halve chicken breasts and pound them between waxed paper. Put chicken thigh meat in bowl of food processor and turn on and off for a few seconds. Add mushrooms, garlic, spinach, and parsley and turn on and off a few times. Add 2 Tbsp. of the white wine, Sherry salt and pepper and egg. Turn on and off until mixture is smooth. Place some of the spinach mixture on each of the chicken breasts and turn in edges to enclose. Either skewer or tie together. Dip in flour, then brown in oil. In another pan saute onion, celery, carrot, and rosemary lightly in butter. Mix remaining wine with tomato paste and stir into vegetable mixture. Season to taste with salt and pepper. Spoon some of the sauce into a heatproof casserole. Place chicken breasts on top. Cover with remaining sauce. Cover and bake in 350' oven for 20 to 25 minutes. Remove cover and bake 5 minutes longer.

*The SOS Column in the L.A. Times came to the rescue for a reader who requested this recipe. The only problem was, the Chef didn't reveal all . . . but we do!*

## VALENTINO'S RIGATONI AL FORMAGGI

12 oz. rigatoni
2 Tbsp. butter
4 oz. Bel Paese cheese, shredded
4 oz. Fontina cheese, shredded
2 oz. Gorgonzola cheese, crumbled
1 cup whipping cream
Grated Parmesan cheese
Ground pepper

Cook pasta according to package directions; drain. Meanwhile, in saucepan melt butter. Add Bel Paese, Fontina and Gorgonzola cheese, stirring till melted. Blend in cream. Place pasta on large platter; add sauce, tossing gently to coat. Sprinkle with Parmesan cheese and ground pepper. Serve at once. Makes 4 to 6 servings.

*Many restaurants prepare this dish . . . but we think this one is the "Creme de la Creme" as did the jolly waiter who told us the secret ingredients.*

## N.Y. CHOCOLATE CHEESE CAKE

24 chocolate waters
4 Tbsp. melted butter
1/2 tsp. cinnamon
3 8-oz. pkg. cream cheese
3 6-oz. pkg. semi-sweet chocolate bits
3/4 cup strong black coffee
6 eggs, separated
1 cup sugar
2 Tbsp. rum
1/4 tsp. salt
1 cup heavy cream
Chocolate curls

Crush wafers with rolling pin or in food processor. Add melted butter and cinnamon. Grease bottom of 10-inch spring form pan and press mixture onto bottom of pan. Set aside. Bring cream cheese to room temperature. Melt chocolate in coffee over low heat or in electronic oven. In mixer bowl, beat egg yolks until sticky; add 2/3 cup sugar and beat until pale yellow and thickened. Gradually beat in cream cheese, a bit at a time and beat until it looks like whipped butter. This takes about 6 - 10 minutes. Beat in rum and salt. In another bowl, beat egg whites until foamy and soft peaks form; add remaining 1/3 cup sugar, a tablespoon at a time. Beat until glossy but not stiff. Set aside. With mixer on low speed, beat coffee chocolate mixture into cheese mixture. Batter will be thin. Then fold in egg whites. Pour into prepared pan. Place in middle shelf of 350' oven and bake 1 hour. Turn off oven and leave cake in oven, door closed, until oven is cold, (this cake will crack as it bakes and sinks when it cools). Whip cream over ice but do not sweeten. Decorate with whipped cream and chocolate curls.

# Old Italian Charm and Flavor

EGGPLANT VINAIGRETTE

VEAL PICCATA LA STREGA

RICCOTA SPINACH SHELLS

FRUIT GLAZED ALMOND CHEESE PIE

## EGGPLANT TOMATO VINAIGRETTE

2 medium eggplants, long
1 jar peeled red peppers or pimientos
1 large red onion
1/4 bunch parsley, finely minced
3 - 4 large tomatoes

*Dressing:*

1/4 cup wine vinegar (or 1/2 lemon juice)
1/2 cup oil
1/2 tsp. sugar
1 tsp. mustard
2 cloves minced garlic
Ground pepper to taste
1 Tbsp. capers
1 tube anchovy paste

Bake eggplants in 450' oven until they blister. Remove from oven, peel and slice into 1/2 inch slices. Put slices in large glass dish. Salt well, set aside for 1/2 hour. Press off excess liquid with paper towels. Cut red peppers in strips. Cut onion into very thin slices and separate into rings. Layer eggplant on tomato slices, then onion rings, parsley, red pepper, repeat. Combine dressing ingredients and pour over stacks of eggplant and tomatoes. Marinate overnight. Makes 8 to 10 servings.

*Henry Winkler's (The Fonz) mother-in-law graciously gave us this recipe many years ago when she attended our class. It has been a favorite ever since!*

## VEAL PICCATA LA STREGA

16 thin veal slices
Flour
Salt and pepper
Clarified butter
Olive oil
1/2 cup dry white wine
2 Tbsp. fresh lemon juice
2 Tbsp. capers
3 Tbsp. butter
2 - 3 lemons, thinly sliced
1 Tbsp. minced parsley

Pound veal very thin between waxed paper. Dust with flour. Season with salt and pepper. In heavy skillet, saute veal in mixture of oil and butter over high heat until lightly browned on both sides. Remove to platter and keep warm. Add wine, lemon juice and capers to frying pan. Reduce wine mixture by a third. Add butter to sauce. Add veal to pan to reheat. Garnish with lemon slices and minced parsley and serve. Makes 8 servings.

*We discovered this popular Italian restaurant when it first opened . . . the atmosphere as well as this recipe, made it one of our favorites.*

# RICOTTA SPINACH SHELLS

32 large noodle shells
1 pint ricotta cheese
1 (8 oz.) pkg. cream cheese
3/4 cup diced Mozzarella cheese
1 cup drained, cooked, chopped spinach
1 egg
1 green onion, minced
Salt and pepper to taste
Marinara Sauce
1/2 cup grated Parmesan cheese

Cook shells in boiling salted water until just tender. Drain. Combine next 6 ingredients and season to taste. Mix well. Stuff shells. Place in single layer in greased shallow baking dish. Cover with Marinara Sauce and Parmesan cheese and bake in 350' oven for 30 minutes. Makes 8 servings.

*Marinara Sauce:*

1/4 cup olive oil or part vegetable oil
2 cloves garlic, minced
1 medium onion, minced
1/2 medium green pepper, chopped
Salt and pepper to taste
1 (1 lb. 12 oz.) can plum tomatoes
1/2 tsp. oregano
1/2 tsp. basil
1 tsp. sugar

Heat oil, add garlic, onion and green pepper and cook until vegetables are soft. Stir in tomatoes, (breaking up with wooden spoon), oregano, basil, salt and pepper to taste, and sugar. Simmer, covered for at least an hour, stirring occasionally.

# FRUIT GLAZED ALMOND CHEESE PIE

3/4 cup soft butter
1/2 cup powdered sugar
1 1/4 cups flour

Cream butter with powdered sugar. Blend in flour to make soft dough. Pat into 12 inch pizza pan. Prick crust with fork and bake in 350′ oven for 20 minutes. Cool.

*Almond Cheese Filling:*

8 oz. package cream cheese
4 oz. almond paste
1/4 cup sugar
1 egg
1/2 tsp. vanilla
1/4 tsp. almond extract

Beat softened cream cheese with remaining ingredients until smooth. Pour into shell and bake in 350′ oven for 10 minutes. Cool, then refrigerate.

*Glaze and Fruit:*

1 can apricot halves, drained
1 can blueberries, drained
1 can pineapple slices, drained
Currant jelly or apricot jam
1 Tbsp. liqueur

Decorate pie with well drained fruit. Melt jelly or apricot jam with liqueur. Spoon over fruit. Refrigerate until serving.

# A Lasting Impression

CHIANTI'S MOZZARELLA MARINARA

RUFFAGE'S MUSHROOM DRESSING

RAPHAEL'S SALTIMBOCCA

RISO VERDE

DOLCE DE TORRONE

## CHIANTI'S MOZZARELLA MARINARA

2 Tbsp. olive oil
1/2 cup finely chopped onion
1 clove garlic, minced
1/2 Tbsp. dried basil
1/4 tsp. oregano and thyme
1 tsp. sugar
1 tsp. salt
1/2 tsp. pepper
2 Tbsp. minced parsley
2 anchovy fillets, diced
1/2 (6 oz.) can tomato paste
2 (1 lb.) cans Italian-style tomatoes

Heat oil in large skillet. Saute onion and garlic for about 5 minutes. Add seasonings and herbs and anchovy pieces and continue cooking and stirring for another minute. Blend in tomato paste. Whirl canned whole tomatoes in food processor for a few seconds until finely chopped. Add to sauce and blend. Cover loosely and simmer for at least 2 hours.

*Mozzarella Fritto:*

8 pcs. Mozzarella cheese
Flour
2 eggs, beaten
Fine cracker crumbs
Salt, white pepper
Oil, for deep frying
Marinara Sauce
8 strips anchovy fillets

Cut cheese into pieces, 2x3x 1/2 inches. Dip each piece of cheese in flour, then in beaten eggs. Season crumbs with salt and pepper and coat cheese completely with crumbs. This can be done in advance and refrigerated. Heat oil to 375'. Place 2 or 3 pieces of cheese at a time in fry basket and deep fry just until crumbs turn golden. Drain in basket. Place cheese on a small plate, top with hot sauce and an anchovy fillet. Makes 8 servings.

## RUFFAGE'S MARINATED LEMON MUSHROOM DRESSING

1 cup chopped mushrooms
1 cup fresh lemon juice
1 Tbsp. brown sugar
1 1/2 tsp. salt
1/2 tsp. ground black pepper
1/2 tsp. marjoram
1/2 tsp. basil
1/2 tsp. oregano
1/2 tsp. garlic powder
1 1/2 cups olive oil

Combine mushrooms with lemon juice. Add seasonings and blend. Beat in olive oil. Mix again before serving over chilled mixed greens. Makes 3 1/2 cups dressing.

*We managed to "pin down" the effervescent host-owner Richard, long enough to share the ingredients (but not the measurements) of this popular dressing. The measurements are to our taste, but you can certainly adjust them to yours.*

## RISO VERDE

3/4 cups minced spinach
1/2 cup minced scallions
1/4 cup minced parsley
3 Tbsp. butter
1 1/4 cups long grain rice
1/2 cup vermicelli
Salt and white pepper to taste
2 1/4 cups chicken stock
1/2 cup grated Parmesan cheese
Pine nuts, to garnish

In a large heavy saucepan, saute spinach, scallions and parsley in butter over low heat for 5 minutes. Stir in rice and vermicelli (that has been broken into small pieces) and salt and pepper and stir mixture until rice is golden. Add chicken stock, bring to a boil. Cover with tight fitting lid and turn heat to low and mixture simmers for 25 minutes or until liquid is absorbed and rice is tender. Toss rice with cheese and sprinkle with pine nuts. Makes 6 servings.

## RAPHAEL'S SALTIMBOCCA

2 lbs. veal scallops (12 slices)
Salt and white pepper
12 thin slices prosciutto
1/4 lb. Fontina imported cheese
  or Gruyere, cut into slices
4 Tbsp. butter
2 Tbsp. oil
1/2 cup dry white wine or Marsala
1 1/2 cups Brown Sauce
1/4 tsp. each sage and basil
1 tsp. tomato paste

Pound veal slices between waxed paper until 1/4" thin. Season with salt and white pepper. Melt butter and oil in large heavy frying pan. Brown meat quickly on both sides, turn frequently for a total of 3 minutes. Place meat on a rimmed baking sheet. Top each piece with a slice of proscuitto and cheese. Heat in 375' oven for 4 minutes or until cheese melts. Pour off any excess fat from frying pan. Add wine and boil rapidly until reduced by half. Add brown sauce, stir in sage, basil and tomato paste and heat through. Spoon sauce around meat to serve. Makes 6 servings of 2 slices each.

*Brown Sauce:*

Saute 1 sliced carrot, 1 chopped onion and 1 chopped stalk of celery in 3 Tbsp. butter until lightly browned. Add 2 Tbsp. flour, cooking and stirring until flour and butter are well-browned. Add 3 cups beef stock or boullion. 1/2 bay leaf, pinch thyme, sprig parsley, 1 minced clove of garlic and salt and pepper to taste. Simmer, partially covered for 1 hour. When sauce is done, strain.

*One of our newlywed students was eating at Raphaels five times a week until we developed our version of her favorite dish. Now she only eats there four times a week.*

## DOLCE DI TORRONE
## (NOUGAT AND CHOCOLATE FROZEN CREAM)

2 pkgs. ladyfingers or
1 sml. sponge cake
1/2 cup Triple Sec liqueur
1/2 lb. almond nougat (torrone)
2 cups heavy cream
1/3 cup powdered sugar
1 tsp. vanilla
4 oz. semi-sweet chocolate, coarsely grated
1 Tbsp. cocoa

Dip ladyfingers into liqueur and line a 2 qt. round bottom bowl with them. Chop nougat fairly fine. Whip cream and fold in powdered sugar, vanilla, grated chocolate and nougat. Spoon half the cream mixture into lined bowl. Stir cocoa into remaining cream and spoon over first layer. Cover top with remaining ladyfingers. Chill for at least 3 hours. Loosen edges and invert mold. Decorate with whipped cream and sugared almonds. Makes 6 to 8 servings. May be frozen.

*Sugared Almonds:*

Put 1/2 cup sliced almonds in bottom of shallow pan. Sprinkle with a little water just to moisten. Sprinkle with a tablespoon of sugar. Bake in 375′ oven until nuts and sugar turn crisp and are golden. Cool completely. Use as garnish.

# The Italian Peasant's Feast

MARINATED BEANS TUSCAN STYLE
ROASTED RED & GREEN PEPPER SALAD
MEAT STUFFED ARTICHOKES
VALENTINO'S PEASANT SPAGHETTI
CHOCOLATE MARZIPAN TORTA

## MARINATED BEANS TUSCAN STYLE

1 (15 oz.) can Great Northern White Beans
1/2 cup olive oil
2 Tbsp. wine vinegar
2 cloves garlic, minced
2 Tbsp. minced shallots
4 leaves fresh sage
Few sprigs fresh oregano
Salt and ground pepper to taste

Drain beans and spoon into cleaned wine flask or glass bowl. Add all ingredients and close top, marinate for 24 hours. Season with salt and pepper to taste.

## ROASTED RED & GREEN PEPPER SALAD

6 large green & red peppers
5 large firm ripe tomatoes, peeled
20 ripe (pitted) black olives
1/4 cup olive oil
1/2 tsp. each salt & pepper
1/2 tsp. oregano
4 cloves garlic, minced
1 Tbsp. finely minced parsley
6 hard cooked eggs, cut in wedges
1 can rolled anchovies

Set whole peppers on a broiler pan and place about an inch from the heat source. Broil turning frequently with tongs, until peppers are well blistered and charred on all sides, about 10-15 minutes. Place peppers in paper bag. Close bag tightly and leave for 15-20 minutes to loosen skins. Strip off skins. Cut peppers lengthwide into 4 pieces and remove stems and seeds. Cut peppers into crosswise 1/2" strips and place in bowl. Halve tomatoes and discard seeds. Cut into bite-size pieces and add to peppers, along with 10 of the olives. In a jar, combine olive oil, salt and pepper, oregano, garlic and parsley. Cover and shake to blend. Stir into pepper mixture. Taste and add more salt and pepper or garlic if necessary. Cover salad and marinate in refrigerator about 4 hours. Garnish with remaining olives, eggs, and anchovies.

# MEAT STUFFED ARTICHOKES

8 - 10 prepared artichokes
1 lb. ground veal
1 lb. Italian sausages, remove casings
1/2 cup seasoned breadcrumbs
2 eggs
1/4 cup cream
3 Tbsp. minced parsley
2 tsp. basil
1 tsp. thyme
2 - 3 Tbsp. minced green onion
Salt and pepper to taste

Saute veal and sausage meat in large skillet until pink disappears. Drain any fat. Combine meat with remaining ingredients. Fill artichokes with sausage mixture. Cover with cream sauce, sprinkle with Parmesan cheese and a few drops of melted butter. Arrange in well buttered ovenproof dish. Bake in 350' oven for 10-15 minutes or until heated through.

*Cream Sauce:*

3 Tbsp. butter
3 Tbsp. flour
1 cup hot chicken stock
1/2 cup heavy cream
2 egg yolks, beaten
3 Tbsp. grated Provolone cheese
Dash nutmeg
Salt and pepper to taste
Parmesan cheese
Melted butter

Melt butter in sauce pan over moderate heat. Blend in flour and cook a minute longer. Take pan from heat, add stock and cream, stirring constantly. Return to heat and continue stirring until sauce comes to a boil. Cook 1 minute longer. Add some of hot sauce to beaten yolks. Stir back into sauce. Add cheese, nutmeg and salt and pepper to taste.

*How to Prepare Artichokes:*

Wash artichokes. Cut off stems and remove outer leaves. Cut off tips of remaining leaves and carefully remove the chokes, leaving heart intact. Rub insides with lemon. Place artichokes in boiling salted water and cook until tender. Drain and dry carefully.

## CHOCOLATE MARZIPAN TORTA

1 tsp. instant coffee powder
2 Tbsp. hot water
4 oz. semisweet chocolate
3 eggs, separated
1/2 cup butter
3/4 cup sugar
3 1/2 oz. almond paste, crumbled
1/2 cup flour
Chocolate glaze (recipe follows)

Dissolve coffee in hot water in top of double boiler. Add chocolate and melt. Can also be done in electronic oven. Beat egg whites just until stiff peaks form. In another bowl beat butter and sugar together until creamy. Beat in almond paste. Add egg yolks, melted chocolate mixture and flour and continue to beat until blended. Fold in beaten whites until just blended. Spread into a greased 8 or 9" flan pan. Bake in 350' oven 30-35 minutes or until top springs back when pressed lightly with your finger. Cool on rack for 10 minutes and remove from pan. Cool thoroughly before frosting.

*Chocolate Marzipan Glaze:*

1 (7 oz. pkg.) almond paste
Apricot jam
2 Tbsp. sugar
6 Tbsp. water
1 Tbsp. butter
4 oz. semisweet chocolate

Roll out almond paste (between wax paper sprinkled with powdered sugar) to 8" round to fit top of cake. Spread cake layer first with heated apricot jam; let set. Then place almond paste round on top of cake. Pat firm. Make glaze by combining sugar and water and bringing to a boil and boil for 3 to 4 minutes, over low flame. Pour into melted chocolate and stir until smooth. Stir butter into mixture and when lukewarm spread over cake.

## VALENTINO'S PEASANT SPAGHETTI

1/4 cup olive oil
2 lg. cloves garlic, crushed
2 med. onions, finely chopped
2 Tbsp. fresh thyme
1 Tbsp. fresh basil
1/4 tsp. fennel, crushed

4 oz. thinly sliced proscuitto, cut in pieces
6-8 lg. ripe tomatoes, peeled, seeded & chopped or
2 cans (28 oz. ea.) whole tomatoes
2 Tbsp. tomato paste
1 tsp. sugar
Salt and pepper to taste

In large heavy skillet, heat oil. Add garlic, onions, thyme, basil and fennel. Cook over medium heat until onions are soft. Add proscuitto and continue cooking for a few minutes. Add ripe tomatoes, tomato paste and sugar and salt and pepper to taste. Continue cooking with lid on for 10 minutes. Serve over cooked spaghetti.

# The Way to a Man's Heart

MUSHROOM CLAM APPETIZER

MONTY'S ITALIAN PEPPER STEAK

CAFE SWISS POTATO FANS

BUTTERY HERB BREAD

APRICOT STRATA

## JUDY'S MUSHROOM CLAM APPETIZER

1 lb. mushrooms, chopped
1 medium onion, chopped
1/4 lb. butter
1/4 cup minced parsley
4 (6 1/2 oz.) cans Gorton's minced clams, drained
Garlic salt, cayenne pepper and seasoned pepper to taste
2 - 3 Tbsp. seasoned bread crumbs
Parmesan cheese
Butter
Clam shells

Saute mushrooms in butter. Add onions and continue cooking until onions are just tender. Add minced parsley, clams and mix with mushrooms and onions. Season to taste with garlic salt, cayenne pepper and seasoned pepper. Add just enough bread crumbs to bind mixture together. Taste again for seasonings. Spoon into shells. Sprinkle with Parmesan cheese and little dabs of butter. May be frozen at this time. Bake in 350' oven until tops are browned and bubbly. Makes 3 dozen.

*A gal who has been with us since our first class . . . gave us this 'first class' recipe.*

## CAFE SWISS POTATO FANS

8 baking potatoes, 4" long, 2" wide
4 Tbsp. melted butter
1 tsp. salt
Paprika
2 Tbsp. dry bread crumbs
3 - 4 Tbsp. Parmesan cheese

Preheat oven to 425'. Place peeled potatoes in bowl of cold water to prevent discoloration. Place one potato at a time on a wooden spoon, and beginning about 1/2 inch from the end, slice down at 1/8 inch intervals. Drop each semi-sliced potato back into the cold water. When ready to roast them, drain the potatoes and pat dry with paper towels. With a pastry brush, generously butter a baking dish large enough to hold the potatoes side by side in one layer and arrange them in it cut side up. Baste the potatoes with 2 Tbsp. of the melted butter, sprinkle them liberally with salt and paprika and set them in the center of the oven. After 30 minutes sprinkle a few of the bread crumbs over the surface of each potato, baste with remaining melted butter and the butter in the pan, and continue to roast another 15 minutes, or until the potatoes are golden brown and pierce easily with tip of sharp knife. Sprinkle Parmesan cheese over the potatoes 5 minutes before they are done.

## MONTY'S ITALIAN PEPPER STEAK

8 (8 oz.) filet mignon steaks
1 large onion, cut julienne
2 large green peppers, cut julienne
12 large mushrooms, sliced
3 cups hot Marinara Sauce
6 Tbsp. butter
1/2 cup Sherry
Dash white pepper
8 slices Mozzarella cheese

Broil steaks to almost the desired degree of doneness. Meanwhile, saute onion, green peppers and mushrooms in butter until crisp-tender. Add Sherry and pepper and heat through. Place one slice of cheese on each steak and place under broiler until cheese is melted. Top each steak with vegetables and Marinara Sauce. Serve at once. Makes 8 servings.

*Marinara Sauce:*

1/4 cup olive oil
2 cloves garlic
1 medium onion
1 lb. 12 oz. can plum tomatoes
1/2 tsp. oregano
1/2 tsp. basil
1/2 tsp. sugar
Salt, pepper

Heat oil, add garlic and onion and cook until onion is tender. Stir in tomatoes that have been finely chopped, oregano, basil, sugar, salt and pepper to taste and simmer 20 minutes, stirring sauce occasionally. If desired, substitute 2 cups chopped fresh tomatoes in place of canned tomatoes.

*It was worth the hour's wait at Monty's to sharpen our taste buds for this famous dish . . . it didn't hurt that the waitress felt guilty and helped us detect the ingredients.*

## BUTTERY HERB BREAD

1 large, unsliced day-old bread
1 cup soft butter
1/3 cup finely minced parsley and chives
1/2 tsp. each dried savory, thyme and garlic salt
1/4 tsp. seasoned black pepper
Sesame seeds or poppy seeds
Parmesan cheese

Trim crusts from top and sides of day-old bread. Cut diagonally into 2 inch crosswise slices, about 2 inches from bottom. Then cut diagonally in opposite directions to form diamonds.

Combine remaining ingredients and spread over cut surfaces, top and sides. Can be wrapped and refrigerated or frozen at this point. When ready to bake, bring to room temperature. Sprinkle with grated Parmesan cheese. Bake in shallow pan at 400' for 18 minutes or until golden.

*This original recipe was broadcast over K.N.X. radio at the request of Chef Mike Roy . . . he knew a good thing when he heard it!*

## APRICOT STRATA

1 (11 oz.) pkg. dried apricots
3/4 cup sugar
6 Tbsp. butter
2 cups graham cracker crumbs
4 Tbsp. chopped walnuts
2 Tbsp. sugar
1 tsp. cinnamon
6 Tbsp. soft butter
3 cups sifted powdered sugar
2 eggs
1 tsp. vanilla
1 cup heavy cream, whipped
Chopped pistachios, walnuts or shaved chocolate

Cook apricots in water, until very tender; drain. Add sugar to hot apricots and stir vigorously to make a puree; set aside to cool thoroughly. Mix melted butter with cracker crumbs, nuts, sugar and cinnamon, press on bottom of 10 inch springform pan. Bake in 350' oven for 8 to 10 minutes. In mixing bowl, cream together soft butter and powdered sugar. Add eggs one at a time and beat until smooth, then add vanilla. Spoon over crumbs in pan and gently spread smooth. Put small spoonfuls of cooled apricots over buttercream layer and top with smooth layer of whipped cream. Sprinkle with pistachios, chopped walnuts or shaved chocolate. Cover and chill at least 8 hours before serving. Makes 12 to 16 servings. Can be frozen or made ahead 2 days without whipping cream.

# The Siesta Supper (A Do-Ahead)

CARLOS 'N CHARLIE'S TUNA DIP

JONGRY JOSE'S JALAPENO CHEESE SPREAD

LOS ARCO'S CRAB ENCHILADAS

LAWRY'S SOUR CREAM TORTILLA CASSEROLE

SCANDIA'S CHOCOLATE MOUSSE CAKE

## CARLOS 'N CHARLIES TUNA DIP

1 (14 oz.) can tuna
1 (6 oz.) jar or can Jalapeno peppers
1 onion, minced
1/2 cup mayonnaise
Chopped cilantro

Mix tuna with chopped Jalapeno peppers. Stir in Jalapeno liquid to taste. Add onion to tuna mixture. Stir in mayonnaise until consistency is smooth. Sprinkle cilantro on top and serve with tortilla chips as a dip.

## LOS ARCOS' CRAB ENCHILADAS

4 Tbsp. butter
4 Tbsp. flour
2 (10 oz.) cans red enchilada sauce
1 cup chicken stock
Oregano
Ground cumin
3/4 lb. crab meat, flaked
8 oz. Jack cheese, shredded
1/2 bunch green onions, finely chopped
Oil
10 - 12 corn tortillas
Ripe olives
Sour cream
Avocado slices
Tomato slices

Melt butter in a heavy skillet. Stir in flour and cook for a few minutes. Stir in enchilada sauce and chicken stock and continue cooking until it comes to a boil and is thickened. Add oregano and cumin or fresh cilantro, minced, to taste. Meanwhile, combine crab meat, cheese and green onions. In another skillet, pour enough oil to cover bottom, heat for a few minutes and then dip each tortilla in hot oil and then enchilada sauce. Put spoonful of filling on one end and roll up. Place seam side down in baking dish that has been covered with enchilada sauce. Spoon sauce over top of enchiladas and bake in 350' oven for 20 minutes. Garnish with sour cream, ripe olives, avocado and tomato slices.

## JONGRY JOSE'S CHEESE SPREAD

4 Tbsp. softened butter
1/2 lb. mild Cheddar cheese, grated
2 Tbsp. minced parsley or cilantro
1 1/2 Tbsp. minced Jalapenos
1/2 tsp. hot pepper sauce
1 Tbsp. Worcestershire sauce

Whip the butter until light and fluffy. Add cheese, parsley, Jalapenos, hot pepper sauce and Worcestershire sauce and beat until smooth. Makes 1 1/2 cups.

## LAWRY'S SOUR CREAM TORTILLA CASSEROLE

1/2 cup chopped onions
2 Tbsp. oil
1 can (1 lb.12 oz.) tomatoes
1 pkg. Lawry's Mexican Rice
  Seasoning Mix or Chili
  Seasoning Mix
2 Tbsp. Salsa Jalapeno
12 corn tortillas
1/2 cup oil
3/4 cup chopped onion
1 lb. Jack Cheese, grated
2 cups sour cream
1 tsp. Lawry's seasoned salt
Lawry's seasoned pepper

Saute onions in oil until tender. Add the tomatoes, Mexican Rice Seasoning Mix and Salsa Jalapena. Simmer for 15 minutes, set aside to cool. Fry the tortillas lightly in small amount of oil, 10 to 15 seconds on each side (do not let them get crisp). Pour 1/2 cup of sauce in the bottom of 13 x 9x 2 inch baking dish. Arrange a layer of tortillas over the sauce (tortillas can overlap). Top with 1/3 of the sauce, onions and cheese. Repeat the procedure twice, making 3 layers of tortillas. Combine the sour cream and salt; spread over cheese to edges of the dish. Sprinkle lightly with seasoned pepper. Bake in 325 oven 25 - 30 minutes. Makes 10 to 12 servings.

*Lawry's will generously give this recipe to anyone who asks . . . and everyone who has it in their patio restaurant asks. We're only too happy to pass it along, too!*

## SCANDIA'S CHOCOLATE MOUSSE CAKE

6 eggs
1 cup sugar
1 cup sifted flour
1 tsp. vanilla
6 Tbsp. butter, melted and cooled

Put eggs and sugar in a large mixer bowl; stir just until combined. Set bowl over a pan containing about 2 inches of simmering water. Let stand for about 5 minutes or until mixture is just warm. Remove bowl from water. Beat egg mixture at high speed on mixer for 8 to 10 minutes. Sift flour and sprinkle 2 Tbsp. at a time over egg mixture, fold in gently, add vanilla and butter. Divide batter into 2 greased, floured 10 inch layer cake pans. Bake in 350' oven for about 20 minutes. Or, using spring form pan, bake at 325' for 40 to 45 minutes, and then divide into 2 layers when cool. Loosen edges and remove from pans immediately. Cool on racks.

*Macaroon Layer Cake:*

8 oz. almond paste
2 egg whites
1 1/4 cups powdered sugar
1/4 cup sugar
1 tsp. almond extract

Beat almond paste with 1/4 of the egg whites until no lumps remain. Then gradually add remaining egg whites, a tablespoon at a time, alternately with granulated sugar and then powdered sugar, and beat until smooth. Grease and line a 10 inch pan with double waxed paper and bake 325' oven for 20 minutes. Cool and remove from pan.

## SCANDIA'S CHOCOLATE MOUSSE CAKE
## (Continued )

*Chocolate Mousse:*

8 oz. melted chocolate
1 1/2 cups whipped cream
1 1/2 cups Creme Patissiere
1 cup Kerns strawberry preserves
Chocolate Curls

Macaroon layer cake or
Macaroon cookies
2 - 3 oz. Orange Curacao
2 cups whipped cream

Add melted chocolate to Creme Patissiere, refrigerate until cool. Then add to whipped cream. Spread first layer of Genoise with strawberry preserves, then layer of Chocolate Mousse. Next put Macaroon layer and sprinkle with Curacao, then preserves, and remaining cake layer. Frost whole cake with whipped cream. Sprinkle with chocolate curls.

*Creme Patissiere:*

1/2 cup sugar
4 Tbsp. cornstarch
Dash salt

2 cups milk or half light cream
4 large egg yolks
1 1/2 tsp. vanilla

Combine first 3 ingredients in 1 qt. saucepan. Add 1/4 cup of the milk and blend well. Heat 1 1/2 cups milk and gradually add to the mixture stirring constantly. Stir and cook over moderately high heat until mixture is very thick as mayonnaise. Remove from heat, add beaten eggs a little at a time. Add vanilla. Cool completely before using. Makes 2 cups filling.

*We sat in awe, watching the pastry chef slather chocolate mousse over tender cake layers . . . and then, miracle, he presented us with the cake!*

# The Mexican Fiesta

SCANDIA'S GAZPACHO

SHRIMP CEVICHE

POLLO VERDE

ARROZ CON ELOTE

SOUTH DAKOTA CHOCOLATE CAKE

## SCANDIA'S GAZPACHO

- 4 large ripe tomatoes, coarsely chopped
- 1 large onion, coarsely chopped
- 1 clove garlic
- 1 large cucumber, peeled and sliced
- 1 green chili pepper, coarsely chopped
- 2 cups tomato juice
- 1/2 cup wine vinegar
- 1 1/2 Tbsp. olive oil
- 1/2 cup white or red wine
- 2 tsp. paprika
- 1 tsp. salt
- Dash pepper
- 1/2 tsp. cumin
- Few dashes hot pepper sauce
- Few dashes Worcestershire Sauce
- Diced, peeled cucumbers
- Diced, peeled avocado
- Diced green pepper
- Diced pimiento
- Chopped chives
- Diced white bread, toasted

Combine tomatoes, onion, garlic, cucumber and chili pepper and let soak in tomato juice 2 hours. Add wine vinegar, oil, wine, paprika, salt, pepper, cumin, hot pepper sauce and Worcestershire. Put in blender container or food processor, using steel blade and blend until smooth. Strain and chill several hours to blend flavors. Add water if too thick. Serve in soup bowls. Place diced cucumbers, avocado, green pepper, pimiento, chives and bread cubes in separate bowls and pass as garnishes for soup. Makes 4 servings.

## HARLEAN'S SHRIMP CEVICHE

- 3 lbs. cooked medium shrimp
- 1 1/2 cups cider vinegar
- 1 clove crushed garlic
- 2 tsp. mustard seed
- 2 tsp. parsley flakes
- 1 tsp. celery seed
- 1/4 cup sugar
- 1/2 cup ketchup
- 1 lb. red onions, thinly sliced
- 1 cup oil
- 1/2 tsp. pepper
- 2 tsp. sweet bell pepper flakes
- 1/2 tsp. cayenne pepper
- 4 1/2 tsp. salt
- 2/3 cups lemon juice
- 1 cup drained Mandarin oranges
- Cilantro leaves

Mix all ingredients together and marinate 2 or 3 hours. Garnish with cilantro. Makes 10 servings.

## POLLO VERDE

8 whole large chicken breasts, split, boned, skinned
1 can whole peeled green chilies rinsed of seeds
1 (8 oz.) pkg. Jack cheese, cut into 1 1/2 by 1/2" fingers
1/2 cup corn oil
4 Tbsp. butter
Seasoned salt and pepper
1 Tbsp. finely minced cilantro
1 1/2 cups Ortega Acapulo Hots or green chili salsa
Salt
1 1/2 cups shredded Cheddar and Jack cheese
1 cup sour cream
1 tsp. minced cilantro
2 ripe avocados, peeled and sliced
1 1/2 cups shredded Jack cheese

Pound chicken breasts between wax paper. Season chicken with salt and pepper. Wrap pieces of chili around sticks of cheese. Lay on inside of chicken breasts; tuck in sides and close with toothpicks. Saute in oil and butter mixture, till golden brown on all sides. Season with salt and pepper and sprinkle with cilantro. Remove to baking dish. In same pan, add Acapulco Hots or chili salsa and heat through. Add shredded cheese, then gradually stir in sour cream and season with salt and pepper to taste. Pour over chicken. Sprinkle with cilantro. Sprinkle with Jack cheese and bake in 350' oven for 45 minutes. When ready to serve, lay slices of avocado on chicken and sprinkle with cilantro. Makes 8 servings.

*This is one of our original creations, as delicious as any restaurant specialty. And if one of them wants to "steal" our recipe, please . . . . . "be our guest".*

## ARROZ BLANCO CON ELOTE

1 1/2 cups long grain rice
2 - 3 Tbsp. oil and butter, mixed
1/3 medium yellow onion, peeled and sliced thin
1 clove garlic, peeled and chopped fine
3 1/4 cups (2 10 1/2 oz. cans) chicken broth
1 cup fresh corn or 1 pkg. 10 oz. size frozen, thawed

Heat oil in a large frying pan. Stir in the rice and keep stirring until all the grains are well coated. Place over high heat and fry, stirring constantly, until the rice just begins to take on a little color. Add the onion and garlic and continue cooking, stirring occasionally, until the rice is pale gold, about 10 minutes.

Add the broth and the corn. Stir until well coated. Reduce the heat to medium and cook, without stirring, until almost all the liquid has evaporated, about 20 minutes. Reduce the heat to low, cover and cook five minutes more. Makes 8 servings.

## SOUTH DAKOTA CHOCOLATE CAKE

2 cups sugar
1/2 cup butter
2 eggs
1 tsp. vanilla
3 sq. unsweetened chocolate, melted
1/2 cup buttermilk
2 cups flour
2 tsp. baking soda
1 tsp. salt
1 cup boiling water
Chocolate Glaze

Cream sugar and butter until well blended. Add eggs, vanilla, melted chocolate and continue beating until smooth. Add buttermilk and flour (that has been combined with soda and salt) alternately to chocolate mixture blending after each addition. Add boiling water and mix until smooth, (batter is thin). Pour into well greased and floured 10" baking pan or 2, 9" baking pans. Bake in 350' oven for 35 - 40 minutes for 9" pans and 45 - 50 minutes for 10" pan. Cool in pan for 10 minutes.

*Chocolate Glaze:*

1/2 stick butter
1 Tbsp. cognac or other liqueur
2 Tbsp. water
3 Tbsp. white corn syrup
1 tsp. instant coffee
Dash salt
4 oz. semi-sweet chocolate

Bring butter, cognac, water, syrup, coffee and salt to a full boil. Remove from heat. Add chocolate, cover saucepan and let stand 5 minutes. Stir, cool until glaze thickens to proper consistency, about like whipping cream. Pour all of the glaze onto the middle of the cake and spread to sides with a spatula.

*At the end of a cooking class when everyone was quietly finishing their dessert . . . this hilarious comment broke the silence "This cake is better than sex!"*

# A "Chili" Winter Dinner

RED ONION'S NACHOS
"OUR" FAMOUS CHILI
ANTONIO'S CALABACITOS RELLENOS
LAS CANTINAS LEMON CAKE
PANCHITO'S MEXICAN COFFEE

## RED ONION'S NACHOS

- 1 doz. corn tortillas
- Oil or lard
- Salt
- 2 cups grated Jack cheese
- 2 cups grated Cheddar cheese
- 2 or 3 Jalapeno chiles, finely minced
- Refried beans
- 1 cup finely diced tomatoes seasoned with salt and pepper
- 1 cup finely chopped cilantro

Cut tortillas in quarters and fry in deep hot oil until crisp. Drain and salt lightly. Arrange tortillas in a single layer on a large platter. Sprinkle half the Jack and Cheddar cheese over the chips. Sprinkle chiles over the cheeses. Dollop generously with refried beans and gently spread beans over tortillas. Now sprinkle with half the remaining cheeses. Top cheese with tomatoes and cilantro, then with the remaining cheeses. Bake at 375' until cheese is melted and bubbly, about 15 minutes. Serve at once. Makes 6 main dish servings or 12 appetizer servings. If desired, garnish with guacamole and sour cream.

## "OUR" FAMOUS CHILI

- 1 lb. ground pork
- 2 1/2 – 3 lbs. chuck roast, blade cut, cut into 1/2" cubes, lightly floured
- 1/4 cup oil
- 2 large green peppers, chopped
- 2 large onions, chopped
- 2 cloves garlic, minced
- 1/4 cup minced cilantro
- Salt and pepper to taste
- 2 tsp. oregano
- 2 tsp. cumin
- 3 - 4 Tbsp. chili powder
- 1 (12 oz.) can tomato paste
- 28 oz. can whole tomatoes
- 1 (7 oz.) can green chile salsa
- 15 oz. can pinto beans (or kidney)
- 8 oz. shredded Jack cheese

Saute pork in hot skillet and drain. Set aside. Heat oil in large skillet and brown meat on all sides. Add green peppers, onions, garlic and minced cilantro and saute for 10 minutes. Add pork and continue cooking for 10 minutes. Season with salt (start with 2 tsp.) pepper, oregano, cumin and chili powder. Stir in tomato paste. Puree tomatoes in food processor (along with juice) and add to meat with chile salsa. Add beans. Taste again for seasonings. Simmer covered for 1 1/2 hours or till meat is tender. Remove cover and continue cooking for 30 minutes, stirring now and then. Stir in cheese and serve. Makes 1/2 gallon.

*We tasted chili from Chasen's, The Magic Castle's and from quite a few friends . . . the girls in the class, voted ours Number One!*

# ANTONIO'S CALABACITAS RELLENOS
## (Chicken Stuffed Zucchini)

2 chicken breasts, poached, shredded
Oil
1/2 medium onion, finely chopped
1 green pepper, cut in thin strips
1 tomato, peeled and chopped
2 cloves garlic, minced
Salt and pepper
6 zucchini
Spanish Sauce
1 cup mixed grated Mozzarella and Jack cheese

Heat oil in skillet. Add onion and green pepper and cook until tender. Add tomato, garlic and salt and pepper and cook, stirring a few minutes longer. Stir in chicken and cook just to heat chicken through. Bring a large pot of water to a boil. Drop in zucchini and cook for 10 minutes. Drain and rinse in cold water. Cut zucchini in halves. Scoop out centers and stuff with chicken mixture. Cover halves with Spanish Sauce. Sprinkle with cheese and bake in 350' oven until cheese is melted, about 10 minutes.

*Spanish Sauce:*

Combine in a saucepan, 2 peeled and chopped tomatoes, 1 chopped onion, 2 stalks finely chopped celery, 1 chopped green pepper, 1 clove minced garlic, 1/4 tsp. cumin, 1 bay leaf, 1 cup chicken stock and salt and pepper to taste. Simmer 30 minutes or until sauce has thickened.

*A favorite eating place of Mexican food aficionados, Antonio's doesn't mind revealing a few secrets . . . this was one.*

## LA CANTINA'S LEMON CAKE

2 cups sifted flour
2 tsp. baking soda
1/2 tsp. salt
1/2 tsp. cinnamon, optional
3 eggs + 1 egg yolk
3/4 cup oil
3/4 cup buttermilk
2 cups sugar
2 tsp. vanilla
1/4 cup lemon juice
2 Tbsp. powdered sugar

Sift dry ingredients together. Beat eggs, add oil, buttermilk, sugar and vanilla and blend together. Add to dry ingredients and mix well. Pour into 9" x 13" well greased pan. Bake in 350' oven 40 to 45 minutes or until toothpick inserted in cake comes out clean. Mix lemon juice and sugar and spoon over cake. Cool in pan; cut into squares and serve with Lemon Sauce.

*Lemon Sauce:*

1/2 cup butter
1 cup sugar
1/4 cup water
1 egg, well beaten
3 Tbsp. lemon juice
Grated rind - 1 lemon

Combine all ingredients in saucepan. Cook over medium heat, stirring constantly till mixture comes to a boil.

*La Cantina keeps this recipe a guarded secret . . . we couldn't, but you should.*

## PANCHITO'S MEXICAN COFFEE

1 oz. Tequila
1/2 oz. Kahlua
1 tsp. grated chocolate
Hot coffee
Whipped cream

Place Tequila, Kahlua and chocolate in mug. Fill with hot coffee and top with whipped cream. Makes 1 serving.

# A New Year's Resolution

SALMON IN HORSERADISH CREAM

BAGEL CRISPS

POPOVER PANCAKE – COOK N' HOLD SCRAMBLED EGGS

SCANDIA'S APPLE CAKE

## SALMON IN HORSERADISH CREAM

8 oz. smoked salmon, shredded
1/2 cup finely minced scallions
2 tsp. fresh minced dill
3/4 sour cream
2 Tbsp. horseradish
1 Tbsp. mayonnaise
Salt and freshly ground pepper

Add scallions and dill to smoked salmon. In a separate bowl, combine sour cream, horseradish and mayonnaise. Season with salt and pepper. Taste and add more horseradish if needed. Add dressing to salmon and toss gently. Serve with rye or pumpernickel crisps.

## SCANDIA'S APPLE CAKE

2 cans apple pie filling
1/4 cup brown sugar
3 to 4 Tbsp. fresh lemon juice
2 cups toasted cake crumbs
3 oz. sliced almonds, toasted
6 oz. currant jelly, stirred
3 oz. nuts, finely chopped
12 macaroons
1 cup heavy cream, whipped and sweetened

Empty apple filling into bowl. Add sugar and lemon juice to taste. Butter heavily the bottom of a 2-inch deep, 9-inch spring form pan. Sprinkle 1/2 cup cake crumbs over bottom of pan. Spread half of the apples over the crumbs. Add 1/2 cup crumbs; top with dollops of jelly, then nuts, then 1/2 cup more crumbs, then macaroons. Top with remaining apples and cover with remaining crumbs. Press down gently with palm of hand to firm. Bake at 375' for 30 minutes. Cool and keep in refrigerator. A few hours before serving, remove from spring form. Decorate with whipped cream and toasted almonds. Makes 12 servings.

*Meeting Henry, the Pastry Chef of Scandia, was a red letter day in our career of "recipe sleuthing". Henry invited us to watch him work one early morning. And, we came away with . . .*

## POPOVER PANCAKES

6 eggs
1 1/2 cups flour
1/4 tsp. salt
1 1/2 cups milk
3/4 cup butter
Cook'n Hold Scrambled Eggs
Sauteed Chicken Livers

Heat oven to 425'. Beat eggs, stir in flour, salt till smooth; gradually stir in milk. Divide butter into two, 10-inch skillets. If handle on skillet is not ovenproof, wrap it with foil to protect from heat. Place in oven until butter melts and starts to bubble. Pour batter into hot skillet. Bake 20 minutes or until puffed and golden brown. Remove from oven. Spoon Scrambled Eggs in center of each puff and surround with Sauteed Chicken Livers. Makes 8 servings.

*Cook'n Hold Scrambled Eggs:*

1/3 cup butter
14 eggs
1 1/2 cups milk
1 1/4 tsp. salt
1/4 tsp. white pepper
2 Tbsp. flour

Melt butter in electric skillet set at 175'. Combine eggs, milk, salt, pepper, and flour in large bowl. Mix with beater until smooth. Pour eggs into skillet. Increase temperature to 250'. Stir eggs from outside edge toward center, allowing uncooked egg in center to flow to outside. Continue stirring until all the egg has cooked and has a creamy appearance. Lower temperature to 170'. The eggs may be covered and held up to 2 hours.

*Sauteed Chicken Livers:*

1 1/2 lb. chicken livers
1 small onion, finely chopped
1 Tbsp. minced parsley
4 Tbsp. butter (or half oil)
Salt and pepper to taste

Wash chicken livers and pat dry. Saute along with onions in hot melted butter in large skillet until pink is gone. Add parsley and salt and pepper to taste.

# A Special Mother's Day Brunch

FRUIT AMBROSIA PARFAIT

MAGIC PAN'S CRISPY HAM CREPES

GRISWOLD'S BRAN MUFFINS

DINAH'S APPLE PANCAKE

HOT MOCHA ORANGE

## ANNABEL'S FRUIT AMBROSIA PARFAIT

1 large can pears, drained, cut into pieces
1 can (8-10 oz.) crushed pineapple, drained, reserve juice
2 1/2 cups miniature marshmallows
1 cup Maraschino cherries, halved
1 cup sour cream
1 cup flaked coconut

2 (3 oz). pkgs raspberry gelatin
2 cups boiling water
2 (10 oz.) pkgs. frozen raspberries
2 to 3 bananas, sliced diagonally
1 cup heavy cream, whipped
2 - 3 Tbsp. powdered sugar
Maraschino cherries

Combine pears, pineapple, marshmallows, cherries, sour cream and coconut and refrigerate overnight. Dissolve gelatin in boiling water. Stir in partially defrosted frozen raspberries. Pour into large glass serving bowl or large brandy snifter and refrigerate until set. Dip banana slices into reserved pineapple juice and put layer of bananas over gelatin layer. Place a row of bananas around inside rim of glass. Spoon in fruit ambrosia mixture and level with spatula. Whip cream and sweeten to taste with powdered sugar. Decorate top of fruit with dollops of cream and garnish with stemmed cherries.

*Even the gourmets who turn up their noses at the mention of "jello molds" will agree this one is truly a winner.*

## MAGIC PAN'S CRISPY HAM CREPES

| | |
|---|---|
| 3 eggs | 1/2 tsp. salt |
| 1 cup flour | 1 1/2 cups milk |
| 2 Tbsp. butter | |

Beat eggs with a fork. Add flour and salt. Continue beating until batter is smooth or place in blender and whirl 30 seconds. Gradually add milk, beating again until smooth. Melt butter and set aside. Before preparing each crepe, brush 8-inch crepe pan with a little butter and heat over medium heat until butter bubbles but doesn't smoke. Remove pan from heat. Pour in 2 Tbsp. batter. Rotate pan so batter covers entire bottom of pan. Return to heat. Cook about one minute, turn and brown other side. Makes 12 to 14 crepes.

*Ham Filling:*

| | |
|---|---|
| 1 lb. ground ham | White pepper |
| 1 cup sour cream | 1/4 cup chopped black olives (opt.) |
| 2 eggs | 8 8-inch crepes |
| 1/2 tsp. onion powder | 3 eggs |
| 2 tsp. Worcestershire sauce | 1 cup milk |
| Salt | Cracker meal |

Mix ham, sour cream, eggs, onion powder, Worcestershire sauce, salt and pepper to taste and olives. Spoon filling on 1/2 of each crepe, forming a rectangle 6 by 1 1/2 inches. Fold filled half over to centerline of crepe, covering filling. Roll up, pressing down lightly on edges so that it holds together and is flattened slightly. Mix eggs and milk together. Dip filled crepes into egg mixture and drain. Roll in cracker meal. Can refrigerate at this point. Deep fry in 350' oil until golden brown. Keep crepes warm in 150' oven until all are fried. Serve with Mustard Sauce.

*Mustard Sauce:*

| | |
|---|---|
| 2 egg yolks | 1 cup salad oil |
| 1/2 tsp. salt | 1 1/2 tsp. lemon juice |
| 1/4 tsp. white pepper | 2 Tbsp. prepared mustard |
| 2 tsp. vinegar | 1 Tbsp. honey |

Place egg yolks in mixing bowl or blender. Beat lightly. Add salt, pepper and vinegar. Blend thoroughly. Pour oil very slowly into eggs while beating continuously at medium speed. Add lemon juice, mustard and honey. Blend again.

## GRISWOLD'S BRAN MUFFINS

1/4 cup butter
6 Tbsp. brown sugar, packed
1 cup sugar
6 Tbsp. honey
1 Tbsp. water
1/2 cup whole wheat flour
1/2 cup plus 2 Tbsp. cake flour
1/2 tsp. salt
1/2 tsp. soda
1/2 tsp. cinnamon
1/2 cup raisins
2 eggs
1/4 cup oil
1/4 cup well drained crushed pineapple
3 cups whole bran cereal
1 1/2 cups buttermilk

Cream butter until fluffy and gradually beat in brown sugar and 6 Tbsp. sugar. Blend in 2 Tbsp. honey and water and whip until fluffy. Coat 12 muffin cups liberally and evenly with mixture, using about a tablespoon per cup. Combine whole wheat flour and cake flour, remaining 10 Tbsp. sugar, salt, soda and cinnamon. Stir in raisins. Add eggs, remaining 1/4 cup honey, oil and pineapple and blend. Stir in bran and buttermilk and mix until batter is smooth. Fill coated muffin pans 3/4 full. Bake at 400' for 18 to 20 minutes. Remove muffins from pans immediately by turning upside down on racks. Makes 12 muffins.

*It was worth an early ride to the desert, to sample and detect the ingredients for this famous muffin . . . as Natalie Houghton featured it and us in a Holiday Brunch in the Valley Times.*

## DINAH'S APPLE PANCAKE

6 eggs
1 1/2 cups flour
1/4 tsp. salt
1 Tbsp. sugar
1 1/2 cups milk
3/4 cup butter
3 large apples, peeled, cored
 thinly sliced
Lemon juice
3/4 cup sugar
2 Tbsp. cinnamon

Heat oven to 425'. Beat eggs, stir in flour, salt and sugar until smooth; gradually stir in milk. (Batter may be made ahead). Divide butter between two 9-inch skillets. If handle is not ovenproof, wrap it with foil to protect from heat. Sprinkle apple slices with lemon juice and divide between the two pans. Divide sugar and cinnamon over apples and saute until glazed and golden. Put pans in oven and divide batter into pans. Bake 20-25 minutes until puffed and golden brown. Serve at once. Makes 8 to 10 servings.

*This has been a famous dish over the years for natives and tourists, alike. It was a labor of love to uncover this recipe.*

## HOT MOCHA ORANGE

1 cup heavy cream
Slivered orange peel
4 cups double strength coffee
4 cups milk
1/2 cup chocolate syrup

Whip cream in a small bowl until stiff; cover and refrigerate until serving time. With a potato parer or citrus stripper, remove thin slices of peel from an orange (do not include white part of peel). Cut slices into very thin slivers. Make four 8 oz. cups of coffee using twice the usual amount of coffee (you can brew your own or use instant). Place in a saucepan, add milk and chocolate syrup. Heat, stirring constantly, just until mixture is hot. Pour into cups or mugs; top with a dollop of whipped cream. Sprinkle with orange slivers. Makes 8 servings.

# Father Deserves The Best

CAFE SWISS DELICE AU GRUYERE

SCANDIA'S MARINATED CUCUMBERS

BEEF MOUTARD WITH FRENCH FRIED ONIONS

L.A. DESSERT'S MARJOLAINE CAKE

## CAFE SWISS DELICE AU GRUYERE

4 Tbsp. butter
4 Tbsp. flour
1 cup milk
2 large whole eggs
2 large egg yolks
2 cups grated Gruyere cheese
1/8 tsp. salt
Dash white pepper
Fine dry bread crumbs
1 large egg, beaten

Melt butter in saucepan, take from heat and blend in flour. Gradually add milk, put back on heat and stir constantly until thickened. Beat in whole eggs and egg yolks, one at a time. Stir and cook over low heat until very thick. Remove from heat; blend in cheese, salt and pepper. Spread in a buttered baking pan. Cover lightly and chill. Shape into rectangles about 1 by 3 inches. Dip in breadcrumbs, then dip in beaten egg, and again in crumbs. Chill for 20 minutes. Brown in deep fat preheated 375'. Drain on paper towels. Makes about 32.

*Tomato Sauce:*

Peel 4 to 6 medium tomatoes and chop. Saute 1/2 medium chopped onion in 1 Tbsp. butter. Add tomatoes, minced parsley, salt and pepper to taste, and a dash of sugar.

*This recipe helped to make Cafe Swiss an institution in Beverly Hills . . . it didn't hurt us either!*

## SCANDIA'S MARINATED CUCUMBERS

Wash 4 large cucumbers. Score lengthwise with a fork and cut them in the thinnest slices possible. Arrange in thin layer in a shallow pan and sprinkle with 2 Tbsp. salt. Allow to stand at room temperature for at least an hour. Drain cucumbers by squeezing a handful at a time; spread out on a paper towel. In a bowl, beat together the 1 1/2 cups white vinegar, 2 Tbsp. sugar, 2 tsp. salt and 1/2 tsp. pepper. Pour over the cucumbers and sprinkle with 4 Tbsp. chopped fresh dill. Chill for 2 to 3 hours and just before serving, drain away nearly all of the liquid. Makes 8 servings.

# BOEUF CREME MOUTARDE

Filet Mignon Roast, cut into 1/2 inch slices

| | |
|---|---|
| Salt and green peppercorns | 2 Tbsp. Dijon mustard |
| 1/4 cup butter | 2 cups sour cream |
| 2 Tbsp. flour | 2 Tbsp. tomato paste |
| 2 cups beef broth | 2 - 3 Tbsp. dill |

Season slices with salt and press in green peppercorns (or cut steak into thin strips and follow same steps), save juice from can of peppercorns. Refrigerate meat for 2 hours. In a saucepan melt butter, add flour and blend. Add broth and stir until sauce is thickened and smooth. Stir in mustard, tomato paste and juice from peppercorns and salt to taste. Add sour cream and dill to sauce just before serving. Heat and pour over meat which has been sauteed in part butter and oil to desired degree of doneness. Garnish with French Fried Onions.

*French Fried Onions*

Peel and slice thinly 4 large white fleshed onions. Separate slices into rings and place in a large bag with 1/2 cup cornstarch and 1 tsp. paprika. Close bag and shake to coat rings evenly. In a deep fryer, heat oil to 360'. Add about 1/3 of the onions to the oil; cook until onions are golden brown. Stir onions frequently. With a slotted spoon, lift browned onions from oil and drain on paper towels; lift out particles that brown faster to prevent scorching. Cook remaining onions, following same procedure. Allow about 1/4 cup per serving. Makes about 8 cups.

## L.A. DESSERT'S MARJOLAINE CAKE

6 oz. each almonds and hazelnuts
1 1/2 cups sugar
8 egg whites
Dash of cream of tartar
Salt

Toast nuts in 350' oven until lightly browned. Cool. Place nuts in bowl of food processor and turn on and off until nuts are finely chopped. (do in 2 batches) Beat egg whites until foamy. Add dash of cream of tartar and salt and continue beating until stiff peaks form. Fold in sugar-nut mixture. Spread in heavily greased 12 by 16 inch baking pan. Bake in 350' oven for 30 minutes, until crusty on top. Cool. Cut into four pieces 4 by 12 inches.

*Buttercream Frosting:*

1 cup sugar
1/2 cup cold water
1/2 tsp. white corn syrup
Dash of salt
8 egg yolks
1 tsp. vanilla
2 1/2 - 3 sticks butter
1/4 cup Praline Powder
3 oz. melted semi-sweet chocolate
3 oz. toasted ground almonds
Powdered sugar

Cook sugar, water and syrup to 242' on candy thermometer. While this boils, add salt to yolks in small mixer bowl. Start beating when syrup reaches 230', beat until light and fluffy. Gradually pour hot syrup into yolks while continuing to beat. Add vanilla. Continue to beat until frosting is completely cool. Cream butter and add to cooled frosting. Combine 1 cup of Buttercream with 1/4 cup Praline Powder; 2 cups of Buttercream with the melted chocolate; 1 cup Buttercream, plain.

## L.A. DESSERT'S MARJOLAINE CAKE
### Continued

*Praline Powder:*

1/2 cup sugar
1/4 cup cold water
1 cup chopped walnuts
Toasted sliced almonds
Powdered sugar

Put sugar and water in small heavy skillet. Stir and cook until sugar dissolves and then stop stirring. Simmer until sugar turns golden. Remove from heat and stir in nuts. Pour mixture on lightly buttered baking sheet. When mixture has hardened (about 30 minutes) break up and grind in food processor or blender.

*Assembling:*

Spread 1 cup of chocolate buttercream on one meringue band, 1 cup praline buttercream on second band and 1 cup plain buttercream on third band. Chill. Place bands of meringue on top of each other and put remaining band on top. Spread remaining cup of chocolate cream around sides of cake. Press sliced almonds on top and sides of cake, and sift powdered sugar over top. Refrigerate until ready to serve.

*Some of our first cooking classes were held at the home of the late Charlotte Irving. She loved to bake and we shared many recipes. It's gratifying to see her children carrying on her tradition in this popular bakery.*

# A Springtime Fancy

MOLDED AVOCADO CREAM

CHICKEN AND MUSHROOMS IN CREPES

GLAZED CARROTS AND GRAPES FOUR SEASONS

LE RESTAURANT'S GLAZED APPLE TART

## MOLDED AVOCADO CREAM

1 envelope gelatin
1/4 cup cold water
1 Tbsp. lemon juice
Seasoned salt
Dash seasoned pepper
2 cups sour cream
1 cup mashed avocado
1/2 tsp. salt
3 Tbsp. finely chopped parsley and chives
Dash tabasco
Bay shrimp
1 (4 oz.) jar red or black caviar, well drained
3 or 4 green onions, thinly sliced

In a pan sprinkle the gelatin over the water; let stand 5 minutes to soften. Heat, stirring, until gelatin is dissolved. Combine all ingredients, except last three and thoroughly blend with gelatin mixture. Pour into 3 - cup mold, cover and chill until set. Garnish top of mold with row of Bay shrimp and row of caviar.

## GLAZED CARROTS AND GRAPES – FOUR SEASONS

1 lb. carrots 1/2
1 Tbsp. brown sugar 1 1/2 t
1 Tbsp. white sugar 1 1/2 t
1 tsp. salt 1/2
3 Tbsp. butter 1 1/2 T
1 Tbsp. flour 1 1/2 t
4 Tbsp. brown sugar 2 T
1/4 cup orange juice 1/8 c
2 Tbsp. Vodka 1 T
1 cup seeded grapes 1/2

Cut carrots in 1 inch diagonal slices. Cook covered in water sweetened with brown and white sugar and salt. Cook until barely tender, about 20 minutes. Drain well. Melt butter in saucepan; add flour and blend; add sugar and then stir in orange juice. Add the grapes and heat through. Add vodka, heat to boiling and serve. Makes 8 servings.

## CHICKEN AND MUSHROOMS IN CREPES

- 6 to 8 whole chicken breasts, skinned and boned
- Butter
- 1/4 cup butter
- 1 lb. mushrooms, sliced
- 1/2 cup minced green onions
- Salt, pepper, thyme, marjoram
- 16 crepes
- Mornay Sauce
- Parmesan cheese

Partially freeze chicken breasts, then slice into thin scallops. Sprinkle with salt and pepper and dust lightly with flour. Saute chicken in butter on both sides until golden. Remove to platter to cool. Add 1/4 cup butter to pan and saute mushrooms and green onions till tender. Season with salt, pepper and pinch of thyme and marjoram.

*To assemble:*

Lay out crepes on work surface, arrange slices of chicken on each crepe, sprinkle each with mushroom mixture and a spoonful of Mornay Sauce. Roll each crepe around filling and place each crepe in buttered baking dish and cover with remaining Mornay Sauce. Sprinkle with parmesan cheese. (May be frozen at this point). Bake in 350' oven for 20 to 25 minutes until golden and bubbly. Makes 8 servings.

*Crepes:*

- 2 cups flour
- 1/4 tsp. salt
- 4 eggs, lightly beaten
- 1 cup milk
- 1 cup water
- 1/4 cup melted butter
- Butter for frying

Place flour and salt into mixing bowl. Gradually beat in eggs with whisk. Add liquids a little at a time, beating after each addition. When batter is smooth, stir in melted butter. Allow to stand in refrigerator for 2 to 3 hours.

Use a 7 or 8 inch crepe pan, brush with butter and place over moderately high heat till pan is hot and butter bubbles, but before butter turns brown. Remove pan from heat, quickly swirl in sufficient batter to cover bottom of pan. Place skillet back on heat, and when top is dry, turn over and cook for few seconds longer and turn onto cloth or counter. Brush skillet with butter again and repeat process. Makes about 3 dozen crepes.

## CHICKEN AND MUSHROOMS IN CREPES
## (Continued)

*Mornay Sauce:*

| | |
|---|---|
| 6 Tbsp. butter | 1 1/2 cups milk |
| 6 Tbsp. flour | Salt, pepper, dash nutmeg |
| 1 1/2 cups chicken stock | 4 Tbsp. each grated Swiss & Parmesan |

Melt butter, slowly blend in flour to make a thick paste; remove from heat and slowly add liquids stirring constantly with a whisk and return to heat. Add salt, pepper and nutmeg to taste and stir over low heat for about 5 minutes or until sauce is very thick, add the grated cheeses.

## LE RESTAURANT'S GLAZED APPLE TART

1 pkg. frozen patty shells
1 cup sugar
1/2 cup water
2 Tbsp. corn syrup
4 Tbsp. butter
6 - 8 medium Rome apples
3 Tbsp. sugar
1 Tbsp. vanilla
1/2 cup apricot preserves or
apple jelly (optional)

Defrost patty shells, stack together and roll out to fit a 10 inch by 2 inch aluminum cake tin. Refrigerate. In a heavy saucepan mix together sugar, water and corn syrup and cook over high flame until mixture becomes light brown. Pour a thin layer of the boiling caramel over the bottom of the pan. Set aside to cool. Put 2 Tbsp. of butter and half the apples (cut into eighths) in a heavy skillet; sprinkle with half the sugar and vanilla and saute 2 - 3 minutes. Set aside to cool, on flat surface. Repeat process with other half of apples, butter, sugar and vanilla. Arrange cooled apple slices (with the outside of the edge of the fruit on the bottom) over caramel in pan. Cover the top of the tart with the refrigerated puff pastry, pressing down dough around edges.

Bake in 425' oven for 45 minutes. Before taking tart from oven be sure syrup is boiling and thick. Cover with foil if crust is too brown. Allow tart to cool 10 minutes before unmolding. Glaze with melted apricot or apple jelly. Garnish with whipped cream if desired.

*A classic French dessert that we made easier to prepare by using frozen puff pastry. No one will know your secret as the caramel sauce defies discovery.*

# The Fish Lover's Delight

MUSSO AND FRANK'S CHIFFONADE SALAD

LE ST. GERMAIN'S TROUT IN RED WINE SAUCE

CREAMED SPINACH IN PASTRY ROLL

LEMON MERINGUE PUFF

# LE ST. GERMAIN'S TROUT IN RED WINE SAUCE

8 trout (8 - 10 oz. each) cleaned
1 1/2 cups finely chopped onions
2 cloves garlic, minced
3 carrots, chopped fine
1/4 cup chopped parsley
1 bay leaf
1/2 tsp. thyme
Few peppercorns
2 tsp. salt
3 cups Beaujolais wine
6 Tbsp. sweet butter, softened
Water
1 1/2 tsp. anchovy paste
1 1/2 tsp. cornstarch
1 pkg. frozen pearl onions
1 Tbsp. butter

Put the onions, garlic, carrots, parsley, bay leaf, thyme, peppercorns, 1/2 tsp. of the salt and wine in a heavy saucepan (not aluminum). Bring to a high boil about 15 minutes or until liquid has been reduced by half. Sprinkle fish with remaining salt inside and out; rub with 1 Tbsp. of the butter. Place fish in shallow baking dish. Pour wine mixture (that has been strained) and enough water to surround fish. Bring to a boil on top of the stove, cover with waxed paper, and put in 425' oven for about 15 minutes. Lift the fish to a heated platter and keep warm. Pour the juices into a saucepan. Place over high heat and reduce by about one-third. Meanwhile, combine the remaining butter and anchovy paste and the cornstarch. Add to the wine mixture with wire whisk. Bring to a boil. Take off the heat at once and combine with pearl onions that have been sauteed in butter until golden and tender. Pour sauce over the fish and serve.

*We were offered "anything" for this recipe by a gourmet Doctor friend. We are still waiting!*

## CREAMED SPINACH IN PASTRY ROLL

- 2 lbs. fresh spinach or
- 2 (10 oz.) pkgs frozen spinach
- 1 cup soft bread crumbs
- 1/2 stick butter
- 2 Tbsp. minced green onions
- 5 Tbsp. flour
- 1 1/2 cups spinach liquid and milk
- 3 egg yolks
- 3 egg whites
- Nutmeg
- 1 tsp. sugar
- 1/2 tsp. dried thyme
- 1/2 tsp. ground black pepper
- 6 to 8 fila dough leaves
- Melted butter
- 1/2 lb. grated Gruyere cheese

If fresh spinach is used, wash and drain it and place it in a saucepan. Cover and cook, without adding water only until spinach has wilted. Press out water and reserve this liquid. Chop spinach fine, add bread crumbs, and set aside. Melt butter, add onion and cook until onion is wilted. Remove from heat and blend in flour. Stir on heat for one minute. Measure spinach liquid and milk to make 1 1/2 cups. Add to the butter and flour. Stir and cook until sauce is thick. Add to spinach and crumbs. Beat egg yolks slightly and add along with the next five ingredients. Mix well. Beat egg whites until they stand in soft stiff peaks, and fold into the mixture. Lay out fila leaves one by one, brushing each with melted clarified butter. Put half the spinach along the side of the dough. Sprinkle with the cheese and then put remaining spinach on top. Turn in sides of dough and then roll jelly roll fashion. Bake in 375' oven for 20 to 30 minutes or until golden brown.

## MUSSO AND FRANK'S CHIFFONADE SALAD

Combine equal amounts of romaine, lettuce and chicory in a large bowl. Add 1 cup finely sliced celery, 3 tomatoes quartered, 3 chopped hard-cooked eggs, 1/2 cup julienne beets and 1/4 cup chopped watercress. Mix with Vinaigrette Dressing by combining: 1/2 cup vinegar, 1 1/2 cups oil, 3/4 tsp. salt, 1 clove garlic, crushed, 1/4 tsp. pepper, 1 Tbsp. each finely chopped green olives, capers, chives, parsley and gherkins.

*They're used to eccentrics in Hollywood, but when we asked for a "baggie" for our leftover salad, the waiter just shook his head in disbelief.*

## LEMON MERINGUE PUFF

6 egg whites
1/4 tsp. salt
1/2 tsp. cream of tartar
1 1/2 cups sugar

Beat egg whites until frothy, add salt and cream of tartar and beat till peaks form. Then beat in sugar, 2 Tbsp. at a time, low speed, continue till very stiff. Heavily butter a 10" pie pan and spread meringue over bottom and up sides to form crust. Bake in 300' oven 30-45 minutes, if too brown, turn down to 275' or 250' and bake till stiff to touch, about 1 1/4 hours. Cool in oven 5 to 10 minutes.

*Lemon Filling:*

6 egg yolks
3/4 sugar
6 Tbsp. lemon juice
2 tsp. finely grated lemon peel
1 cup whipping cream
Lemon slices

In top of double boiler, beat eggs until thick and light in color. Beat in sugar, lemon juice and peel. Cook over boiling water till thick, about 10 minutes. Cool. Whip cream and fold in. Garnish with whipped cream and thin lemon slices.

*This "original" recipe found its way to a well-known caterer. Now, "his" original recipe is a big hit with the movie crowd . . . especially George Segal!*

# The V.I.P. Dinner

PAPADAKIS STUFFED GRAPE LEAVES

LAMB CHOPS CHARLES

RAMEQUIN FORESTIERE

CURRIED FRUIT

MR. A'S CARROT CAKE

## PAPADAKIS TAVERNA DOLMAS
### (Stuffed Grape Leaves)

1/2 cup oil
3 large onions, finely chopped
1 cup long grain rice
1 cup minced parsley
1/4 cup pine nuts (optional)
Salt and pepper to taste
48 grape leaves, washed, drained
2 to 3 Tbsp. fresh lemon juice
2 Tbsp. olive oil

Heat oil in skillet and saute onions until soft and transparent. Add rice and cook for 20 minutes. Add parsley, nuts, salt and pepper; simmer for 5 minutes or until liquid is absorbed. Cool slightly before stuffing leaves. In the center of each leaf, shiny side of leaf down, place a teaspoon of the filling. Fold sides over and starting at stem end, roll up. Place rolls in a shallow, heavy pan, side by side. Sprinkle with lemon juice and olive oil and half cover with hot water. Place a heat proof plate over them to keep rolls from opening. Simmer on a low flame for about 35-45 minutes. The water should be almost absorbed. Cool dolmas, before serving. Brush with oil and surround with lemons.

*Between hands clapping and glass breaking, we plied this recipe from our dancing waiter.*

## HOT CURRIED FRUIT

1 lb. 14 oz. can freestone peaches, drained and save juice
1 lb. 14 oz. can Bartlett pear halves, drained
1 lb. 14 oz. can apricot halves, drained
1 can pineapple chunks, drained
2 tsp. grated lemon peel
Curry powder to taste

Arrange fruit in ovenproof glass dish, about 12 x 8 x 2 inches. Pour one cup of the reserved juice over the fruit. Bake in 450' oven for 20 to 25 minutes. Cover dish with foil and continue cooking at 350' for about 1 hour adding more juice as needed. Serve hot. Makes 8 servings.

## LAMB CHOPS CHARLES

16 lean rib chops
3 slices proscuitto, minced
1 large chicken breast, finely chopped
2 shallots, finely chopped
4 Tbsp. butter
4 large mushrooms, chopped
Pinch thyme, salt, pepper
1/2 tsp. dried tarragon
Ground black pepper
1 cup dry white wine
Fila dough
Melted butter

Season lamb chops and broil to medium on both sides. Drain and cool. Saute proscuitto, chicken, mushrooms and shallots in butter. Season with thyme, salt and pepper. Cook for 5 minutes and remove to a plate. Simmer tarragon and pinch black pepper in 1/2 cup of wine. Continue cooking for another 10 minutes. Spoon meat mixture on each chop. Layer and butter 3 sheets of fila dough. Cut into 4 long strips. Repeat for 16 strips. Wrap each strip around chop. Brush with butter. Can refrigerate covered, at this point. Bring to room temperature and bake uncovered in 375' oven for 25 to 30 minutes. Makes 8 servings.

*From the moment Charles, of San Francisco fame, kissed your hand, the food was an anti-climax . . . except for this fantastic dish which one of our students served at eighteen dinner parties!*

## RAMEQUIN FORESTIERE

1/2 cup flour
2 cups cold milk
3 1/2 Tbsp. butter
1/2 tsp. salt
Dash nutmeg
4 eggs
1 1/3 cups coarsely grated Swiss cheese
1 Tbsp. milk
Spinach Filling

Place flour in saucepan and gradually beat in the milk with a wire whisk. Stir slowly and constantly over moderately high heat until mixture comes to a boil and thickens. Remove from heat; beat in butter, seasonings, and one by one, the eggs. Then beat in 1 cup of the cheese. Turn half the mixture into buttered dish, spread the creamed spinach on top, and cover with the rest of the cheese mixture. Sprinkle on the remaining cheese and distribute the butter over cheese. Refrigerate until ready to bake. Bake in upper third of oven for about 45 minutes at 400'. Makes 8 servings.

*Filling:*

1 (10 oz.) pkg. chopped spinach, cooked and drained
1 1/2 Tbsp. butter
1 Tbsp. finely chopped onion
1 Tbsp. flour
4 - 6 Tbsp. heavy cream
Salt and pepper

Saute onions in butter till soft and golden. Sprinkle in flour and stir for a minute to cook the flour. Remove from heat, pour in the cream, then stir over moderate heat until cream has thickened. Season with salt and pepper. Fold in spinach. Set aside.

## MR. A'S CARROT CAKE

2 cups sifted flour
2 tsp. baking soda
2 tsp. cinnamon
1/2 tsp. salt
3 eggs
3/4 cup oil
3/4 cup buttermilk
2 cups sugar
2 tsp. vanilla
1 sml. can crushed pineapple, drained
2 cups grated carrots
3 1/2 oz. coconut
1 cup chopped nuts

Sift dry ingredients together. Beat eggs; add buttermilk, sugar, oil and vanilla. Mix together. Add to dry ingredients, blending well. Mix in pineapple (reserve juice), carrots, coconut and nuts. Pour into two, well greased 9 or 10 inch cake pans. Bake in 350' oven 55 minutes. Pour following glaze over hot cake.

*Glaze:*

1 cup sugar
1/2 tsp. soda
1/2 cup buttermilk
1/4 lb. butter
1 Tbsp. corn syrup
1 tsp. vanilla

Combine first 5 ingredients in saucepan. Bring to a boil; turn heat down and simmer 5 minutes. Remove from heat and add vanilla. Spoon carefully over cakes in pans. After cakes are cool remove from pans. Put together with a Pineapple Cream Cheese Frosting.

*Pineapple Cream Cheese Frosting:*

1 (3 oz.) pkg. cream cheese, softened
3 to 4 Tbsp. pineapple juice
4 to 5 cups powdered sugar
1 tsp. vanilla

Combine ingredients in bowl. Mix until light and fluffy. Add more juice if necessary. Pay layers together and frost tops and sides of cake. Refrigerate cake until serving time.

*Rumor has it that the chef turned down five thousand dollars for this recipe which we uncovered for much, much less.*

# A Dinner for Thanksgiving

CAVIAR TART CZARINA

SOUFFLEED TURKEY

APPLES WITH YAMS     PORTLY PLUM PUDDING

PUMPKIN CHEESE PIE

FARMERS BISHOP

## CAVIAR TART CZARINA

6 - 8 eggs, hard cooked
6 Tbsp. butter
1 pt. sour cream
Ground pepper
1 Tbsp. grated onion
1 sml. jar caviar, red or black
Cucumbers
Cocktail pumpernickel

Grate the eggs. Melt the butter and add to the eggs. Add some fresh black pepper and grated onion. Press into 9 inch pie plate and put into freezer for 30 minutes after a layer of sour cream has been spread on top of the grated eggs. Remove from freezer and border with a thin layer of caviar. Refrigerate until set. Slice cucumbers to be used as crackers or serve with cocktail pumpernickel bread.

*Although the following group of recipes hasn't appeared on any famous menus, we've taught them to our classes with oustanding success . . . Thanksgiving with a gourmet touch!*

## APPLES WITH YAMS

2 lge. yams
2 Tbsp. butter
Salt and pepper to taste
Grated lemon peel
8 large tart apples
1/4 tsp. cinnamon
1 cup sugar
1/2 cup water
1 1/2 tsp. grated orange peel
8 tsp. butter

Wash yams and bake in 400' oven for 1 1/2 hours or until soft. Cut yams in half and scoop out pulp. Puree yams, adding butter and salt, pepper and lemon peel to taste. Core apples, leaving bottoms intact. Peel the top half of each apple. Sprinkle each cavity with 1/4 tsp. cinnamon. Fill apples with yam puree mounding it on top.

In a saucepan, combine sugar, water and orange peel; bring to a boil over moderate heat. Put apples in heat-proof dish. Pour in syrup. Top each apple with 1 tsp. butter. Bake in 350' oven, basting every ten minutes, for 45 minutes to one hour or until tender.

## CRANBERRY SOUFFLEED TURKEY

- 1 13-16 lb. fresh turkey
- 1 tsp. salt
- 1/2 tsp. pepper
- 1/2 tsp. garlic salt
- 1/2 tsp. seasoned salt
- 2 - 3 stalks celery
- 1 lge. onion, peeled
- 1 orange, quartered

Combine seasonings and sprinkle cavity of turkey. Fill the cavity with onion, celery and orange and truss. Starting at the cavity, breast side up gently force your fingers under the skin and loosen the skin all the way to the neck and down the sides, including as much of the legs as you can reach. Do not loosen skin on back. Stuff with the following mixture:

Combine 9 cups soft bread crumbs, 1 cup coarsely chopped cranberries, 1/4 cup finely chopped parsley, 1/2 tsp. each thyme, savory, 1 1/2 Tbsp. salt, 1/2 tsp. pepper, 1/2 tsp. paprika.

In a skillet, saute 1 cup each of chopped onion and celery in 1 1/2 sticks butter until vegetables are limp. Stir vegetables into bread mixture. Separate 6 eggs. Beat egg yolks and add to bread mixture. Beat egg whites until stiff and gently add to stuffing.

Stuff turkey under the skin and in neck cavity, closing neck cavity. Baste with the following: Blend 1 stick melted butter, 1 tsp. each salt, seasoned pepper, seasoned salt and paprika and 3 cloves crushed garlic. Roast in 325' oven for 3 1/2 to 4 hours.

## PORTLY PLUM AND CARROT PUDDING

1 cup golden raisins
1/2 cup apple cider or rum
1/2 cup butter
1/2 cup sugar
2 cups finely grated carrots
1 cup flour
2 tsp. baking powder
1 tsp. cinnamon
1/2 tsp. salt
2 eggs, well beaten

Soak raisins in cider for one hour. In a bowl cream together butter and sugar. Add grated carrots, raisins and cider. Sift together flour, baking powder, cinnamon and salt and add it to the carrot mixture. Fold in eggs. Pour mixture into well buttered 1 qt. souffle dish or 10 small molds. Bake in 350' oven for 30 minutes or until cake tester inserted in center comes out clean. Serve pudding warm with Rum Sauce and a large pitted prune in center of each pudding. Makes 8 to 10 servings.

*Rum Sauce:*

In a saucepan, combine 1/4 cup sugar and 2 Tbsp. cornstarch. Blend in one cup cold water. Cook the mixture over moderate heat stirring until it is thickened. Remove pan from heat and stir in one cup orange juice and 1/2 cup rum and 1 Tbsp. butter. Cook sauce, stirring for 5 minutes longer.

## FARMER'S BISHOP

6 oranges
Cloves
1/2 of fifth bottle heated rum
(or to taste)
1/2 cup sugar
1/2 gal. cider
Cinnamon
Freshly grated nutmeg

Bake the oranges (each stuck with cloves) in a 350' oven until the juice begins to flow. Put the oranges in flame proof punch bowl. Add heated rum and sugar. Ignite the rum. After a few seconds pour in heated (but not boiled) cider. Season punch with cinnamon and nutmeg to taste. Stir well before serving.

*This drink will become a tradition . . . it's that delicious!*

## PUMPKIN CHEESE PIE

1 3/4 cups crushed graham crackers
1/2 cup finely chopped pecans
1/3 cup sugar
1 Tbsp. cinnamon
1/2 cup butter, melted
1 (8 oz.) pkg. cream cheese
1/2 cup sugar
2 eggs
1 (16 oz.) can pumpkin
3 egg yolks
1/2 cup brown sugar
1/2 cup eggnog
  or half & half
1/2 tsp. salt
2 tsp. cinnamon
1 env. unflavored gelatin
1/4 cup cold water
3 egg whites
1/4 cup sugar
Sweetened whipped cream

Combine crumbs, pecans, sugar, cinnamon and melted butter. Pat into 10 inch spring form pan. Bake in 375' oven 10 minutes. Turn oven down to 350'. In the meantime, beat cream cheese, sugar and eggs until fluffy. Pour over crust and bake 20 minutes. Cool.

Beat pumpkin, yolks, 1/2 cup sugar, eggnog, salt and cinnamon in heavy saucepan. Stir frequently until thick about 5 minutes. Sprinkle gelatin over cold water in saucepan. Stir over low heat, just until dissolved. Stir into pumpkin mixture. Cool. Beat egg whites until foamy. Gradually beat in sugar and beat until stiff peaks form. Gently fold into cooled pumpkin mixture. Pour over cheese filling. Refrigerate. Garnish wtih sweetened whipped cream.

# The Holiday Dinner Supreme

LE. ST. GERMAIN'S MUSHROOM SALAD

CHAMBORD'S ROAST DUCK WITH PEARS

RICE TIMBALES

GATEAU AUX NOIX

## LE ST. GERMAIN'S MUSHROOM SALAD

1 1/2 lbs. mushrooms, cleaned and sliced
1/2 tsp. salt
1/2 tsp. ground black pepper
1 Tbsp. Grey Poupon mustard
1 tsp. Amora mustard
2 Tbsp. Dessault red wine vinegar
3 Tbsp. red wine
10 Tbsp. peanut oil
Minced parsley

Combine salt, pepper, white pepper, mustard, Amora mustard and mix to blend well. Add vinegar and wine and beat until smooth. Gradually add oil and beat until dressing coats a silver spoon. Serve with sliced mushrooms and minced parsley in bibb lettuce cup.

*They may not have been the first to serve this salad but it must be one of the best . . . since it's among one of our most requested recipes.*

## RICE TIMBALES

3 Tbsp. butter
1 small onion, finely chopped
1 clove garlic, minced
1 cup long grain rice
1 tsp. saffron filaments
2 cups chicken stock
1 tsp. salt
1/2 tsp. seasoned pepper
2 Tbsp. minced parsley
2 Tbsp. butter, melted

Melt butter in heavy skillet with a tight lid. Saute onion for a few minutes until tender but not brown. Add garlic and rice and stir until rice is coated with butter. Pour in the stock to which you've added the saffron. Add salt and pepper. Bring to a boil. Put on lid and turn heat to simmering. Cook for 25 minutes. Fluff rice and add melted butter and minced parsley. Pack into 8 small greased molds. Pack firmly. Let molds set for a few minutes before tipping them out.

## CHAMBORD'S ROAST DUCKLING WITH PEARS

5 lb. duck
Salt and pepper
4 fresh pears
2 cups red wine
2 cups water
1/2 cup sugar
1 tsp. nutmeg
1 Tbsp. cornstarch
Salt and pepper
Pear liqueur

Clean duckling. Season with salt and pepper inside and out. Prick the skin all over to allow fat to run out. Roast in 400' oven for an hour. Lower heat to 350' and continue to roast for 30 minutes longer. Peel pears, cut in half and remove core. Poach in a broth made by combining wine, water, sugar and nutmeg. Poach about 20 minutes until tender. Remove from broth to platter and keep warm. Thicken broth with cornstarch mixed with a little water to a smooth paste. Add salt and pepper to taste. Add 1 to 2 Tbsp. Pear liqueur. At serving time, place duck on a warm platter, add two pear halves on top and remaining pears in a circle. Serve carved duck with the pears and sauce. Makes 4 servings.

*A freelance food columnist and student of ours, Barbara Lenox, did the foot work in detecting this recipe and then graciously shared it with us.*

# GATEAU AUX NOIX
## (Walnut and Caramel Filled Torte)

1 1/2 cups sugar
1/2 cup water
1 lb. chopped walnuts
1 3/4 sticks softened butter
1 cup less 2 Tbsp. milk
1/3 cup honey

In a deep heavy skillet combine sugar and water and cook the syrup stirring until the sugar is dissolved. Increase the heat to high and boil the syrup until it is a light caramel. Remove pan from heat and add walnuts, butter and milk. Bring the mixture to a simmer over moderate heat, stirring, simmer it for 15 minutes, and stir in honey, set aside, cool slightly. Roll reserved dough into an 11 inch round on a lightly floured surface. Spoon the nut mixture into the pastry shell. Brush the pastry overhang with water, drape the pastry round over the rolling pin, and arrange it over the filling, pressing the top and bottom crusts together firmly. Cut away any excess dough. Cut a slit in the center and bake the pastry in 425' oven for 20 minutes or till brown. Let the pastry cool for at least 4 hours. Invert cake onto a serving platter, remove ring and glaze.

*Pate Brisee: (sweet crust)*

2 1/2 cups flour
1 1/2 sticks butter
1/4 cup cold shortening
3 Tbsp. sugar
6 Tbsp. ice water

Put half of flour in bowl of food processor. Cut half of butter in 4 slices over flour. Add half of shortening. Turn on and off until mixture resembles coarse corn meal. Add 1/2 water through funnel and run until mixture forms dough. Repeat with remaining ingredients and chill for one hour. Roll 2/3 of the dough into a 12 inch round on lightly floured surface. Fit into a 11 inch flan ring set on baking sheet. Chill for 30 minutes.

*Chocolate Glaze:*

6 oz. semi-sweet chocolate
1/2 stick butter, softened
3/4 tsp. vegetable oil
pinch salt

In top of double boiler set over hot but not boiling water, melt chocolate. Remove the pan from the heat and beat in butter, a little at a time, oil and salt. Spread sides and top cake with chocolate mixture and decorate the top with chopped walnuts around edge. The cake can be kept for up to 2 weeks, refrigerated.

*If you want to make a dessert that's being served at many of the "in" dinner parties around L.A., then try this recipe we uncovered from a famous gourmet publication. Michael's of Santa Monica discovered it, too!*

# Our "Class" Favorite

**KAVKAZ CHEESE BEUREKS**
**MOUSSAKA**
**BULGAR PILAF**
**ARMENIAN SALAD**
**MARZIPAN APRICOT TORTE**

## KAVKAZ CHEESE BEUREKS

2 (8 oz.) pkg. cream cheese, softened
1/2 lb. feta cheese, crumbled
1 egg
1 pkg. refrigerated fila dough
1 cup sweet butter, melted

Blend cheeses together with egg until smooth. Place one sheet of fila pastry on flat, smooth surface; brush with melted butter. Cut lengthwise into strips about 2 inches wide. Put 1 tsp. filling at end of strip. Fold over one corner to opposite side, to make a triangle. Continue folding, keeping triangle shape, to other end of strip. Arrange filled triangles on ungreased cookie sheet. Brush tops lightly with butter. Repeat with other pastry leaves. Bake 20 minutes in a 350' oven. Serve hot. May be frozen, unbaked, on trays, then transferred to plastic bags. When ready for use, bake frozen Beureks in 375' oven for 20 to 25 minutes or until brown and puffy. Makes 6 dozen appetizers.

*A specialty in many middle eastern restaurants and homes, the secret of this recipe was first given to us by the talented wife of a well known Armenian Judge.*

## ARMENIAN SALAD

1 medium red onion, sliced thin
5 to 6 cucumbers, peeled and sliced
1 green pepper, slivered
6 large tomatoes, peeled and chopped
1/4 cup parsley, minced
1/2 cup fresh lemon juice
1/4 cup oil
Salt and pepper to taste

Combine all the ingredients and keep in covered container. Can be made day in advance. Makes 8 servings

# MOUSSAKA

2 eggplants, long rather than wide
Oil
Garlic

Cut eggplant into 1 inch slices, salt and leave for 1/2 hour. Pat dry. Brush both sides of eggplant with oil and season with garlic salt. Place in shallow baking dish and bake in 450' oven for 10 minutes. Turn and continue baking another 10 minutes. Meanwhile prepare meat and cheese sauces.

*Meat Sauce:*

2 lbs. ground round
2 med. chopped onions
1/4 lb. chopped mushrooms
1/4 cup parsley
1 can tomato sauce
2 tsp. salt
1/2 cup red wine
1/8 tsp. cinnamon
Pinch Mayacamas Herb Mix
3-4 Tbsp. fine bread crumbs

Brown meat with onions and mushrooms, add the remaining ingredients and blend together. Set aside to cool.

*Cheese Sauce:*

6 Tbsp. butter
6 Tbsp. flour
2 cups milk
4 egg yolks
4 Tbsp. parsley
6 oz. Feta or cream cheese
Salt and pepper if desired

Melt butter in saucepan and blend in flour. Gradually blend in milk, stirring constantly. Cook until thickened. Beat egg yolks slightly, stir in some of the hot sauce and then stir back into sauce along with parsley and cheese. Cook 5 minutes longer and continue stirring. Season with salt and pepper if necessary.

*To Assemble:*

Arrange 8 eggplant slices in buttered baking dish. Divide cooled meat sauce over each slice. Spread with thin layer of cheese sauce. Repeat with eggplant slice and remaining cheese sauce. Sprinkle with Parmesan cheese and 1/3 cup pine nuts. Bake uncovered in 375' oven for 35 minutes until hot and bubbly. Let cool 5 minutes and serve.

# MARZIPAN APRICOT TORTE

*Pastry:*

1 1/2 cups flour
1/4 cup shortening
1/4 cup butter
2 Tbsp. sugar
1 egg yolk
1 Tbsp. ice water

Place flour in mixer bowl. Add shortening and butter which has been cut into small pieces. While mixer is at low speed, add sugar, egg yolk and water. Gather dough together and refrigerate until needed.

Roll dough over flan ring on cookie sheet. Bake blind 15 minutes (lay sheet of foil over crust and line with beans). Remove beans and continue baking until crust is golden. Cool. Fill cooled flan shell with Marzipan Filling and bake in 350' oven for 25 - 30 minutes or until light brown. Cool and add topping.

*Marzipan Filling:*

1/2 cup butter
1 (8 oz.) can almond paste
2 eggs
2 tsp. flour
4 Tbsp. apricot brandy
Grated peel of one lemon

Cream butter. Add almond paste and beat until smooth. Add eggs, one at a time and continue beating, until smooth. Blend in flour, brandy and lemon peel. Set filling aside.

*Topping:*

1 lge. can apricot halves, drained
3/4 cup strained apricot preserves, heated
1 Tbsp. Brandy
Whipping cream
Pistachio nuts

Place drained and patted dry apricot halves on top of tart. Add brandy to strained preserves, blend and spoon over top. Sprinkle pistachio nuts around border. Serve with whipping cream if desired.

# A Candlelight Dinner

BUTTERFIELD'S MUSHROOM BISQUE

THIRD FLOOR NUT CRUSTED RED SNAPPER

SPINACH SOUFFLEED TOMATOES

EMPEROR'S LEMON TORTE

## BUTTERFIELD'S MUSHROOM BISQUE

- 1/3 cup chopped leeks
- 2 cups button mushrooms, washed, trimmed and drained
- 3 Tbsp. butter
- 6 Tbsp. flour
- 2 1/2 cups chicken stock
- 1/3 to 1/2 cup white wine
- 1 cup heavy cream
- Salt, pepper thyme and Sherry to taste

Saute onion and mushrooms in saucepan over moderate heat until onions are soft. Stir in flour and continue cooking for a few minutes. Take off heat and blend in chicken stock and wine. Return to heat and continue stirring until mixture comes to a boil. Turn heat to low, add cream and seasonings and Sherry to taste. Makes 6 - 8 servings.

*Rudy Butterfield's wife wouldn't give us this recipe . . . but Rudy did!*

## SPINACH SOUFFLEED TOMATOES

- 8 large tomatoes
- 1 (10 oz.) pkg. frozen spinach, thawed
- 1/2 cup finely chopped onion
- 2 Tbsp. butter
- 4 eggs, separated
- 1 cup half and half
- 1 1/2 cups grated Cheddar cheese
- 1 Tbsp. anchovy paste
- Salt, pepper, nutmeg
- 8 partially baked, prepared tart shells

Cut slice from top of tomatoes. Scoop out inside of tomatoes, drain tomato shells. Melt butter in skillet. Add tomato pulp, spinach and onion and simmer uncovered over medium heat until moisture has evaporated. Heat cream until a film forms on top. In a medium bowl, beat egg yolks until light and thick. Add heated cream gradually and pour back in saucepan. Simmer over low heat, stirring constantly, until custard thickens and coats a spoon. Remove from heat. Stir in tomato mixture, cheese, anchovy paste and salt, pepper and nutmeg to taste. Cool.

Beat egg whites until stiff. Fold into tomato mixture. Spoon filling into tomato shells. Place tomatoes in tarts and spoon remaining filling around tomatoes. Bake in 400' oven 15 minutes. Turn heat down to 300' and bake 10 - 15 minutes longer. Makes 8 to 10 servings.

## THIRD FLOOR NUT CRUSTED RED SNAPPER

8 - 10 Red Snapper fillets
  8 - 10 oz. each
Lemon Juice
1 cup coarsely chopped Macadamia
  nuts (pecans or almonds)
1/2 cup fine dry bread crumbs
2 Tbsp. minced parsley
1/4 tsp. pepper
2 eggs, beaten
Flour
6 Tbsp. each butter
  and oil

Sprinkle fish with lemon juice, salt and pepper. Combine on a plate nuts, bread crumbs, parsley, salt and pepper. In a shallow pan, beat eggs together. Dip each fish into flour, then beaten eggs, then into nut mixture to coat all over. Set aside.

Put butter and oil in large shallow baking pan and put in 500' oven until butter melts. Take from oven and lay one fish in pan, turn to coat with melted butter and oil and repeat with remaining fish, arranging in a single layer in pan. Return to oven and bake until fish is golden brown and flakes in the thickest portion, about 12 minutes. Makes 8 servings.

*Save yourself the air fare to this fabulous Hawaiian restaurant, by preparing our unusual recipe at home . . . or better yet, send copies of this book to all your friends, so we can go back again.*

## EMPEROR'S LEMON TORTE

| | |
|---|---|
| 2 cups flour | 2 egg yolks |
| 3/4 cup butter | 2 Tbsp. cream |
| 3/4 cup sugar | 1 tsp. grated lemon peel |

Mix flour and butter in food processor or bowl until it resembles corn meal. Add sugar, egg yolks, cream and lemon peel and run until dough leaves side of bowl, or work with hands until soft dough forms. Refrigerate if necessary. Roll dough between waxed paper to cover bottom and 1 1/2 inches up the sides of a 9 inch greased spring form pan. Keep out enough dough to make 6 strands for top of cake. Spoon in Almond Filling. Criss cross top of cake with dough strands and press into sides. Bake at 350' for 30 minutes or until golden. When cooled, fill spaces with Lemon Filling.

*Almond Filling:*

| | |
|---|---|
| 3 egg whites | 1 1/3 cups coarsely ground almonds |
| 1 cup sugar | |

Whip egg whites until stiff peaks form. Fold in combined sugar and ground almonds.

*Lemon Filling:*

| | |
|---|---|
| 5 egg yolks | 2 large lemons, juice and grated rind |
| 1/2 cup sugar | 1/4 cup sweet butter |

In a heavy saucepan or top of double boiler, combine egg yolks and sugar over low heat. Add lemon juice and rind. Stir, adding butter little by little. Cook until thick, stirring constantly. Garnish finished cake with toasted sliced almonds and powdered sugar. Makes 8 to 10 servings.

# The Fare Extraordinaire

CHILLED ZUCCHINI SOUP

MON GRENIER'S SALMON IN PUFF PASTRY

ASSORTED PUREED VEGETABLES

POACHED PEARS

L'ERMITAGE'S CUSTARD SAUCE

# MON GRENIER'S SALMON IN PUFF PASTRY WITH BEARNAISE SAUCE

8 salmon steaks
Court Bouillon
2 cups white wine
1/2 cup chopped onion
1/2 cup chopped carrot
1/2 cup chopped celery
2 tsp. salt
8 peppercorns
3 sprigs parsley
1 bay leaf
1 clove
1/4 tsp. thyme
2 qts. water
Mushroom Duxelles
Quick Puff Pastry
Bearnaise Sauce

*Court Bouillon:*

Put all ingredients for Court Bouillon into a large saucepan and boil for 1/2 hour. Strain through cheesecloth and cool. Put rack on bottom of large skillet (or wrap steaks in cheese-cloth). Place fish on rack. Pour cooled Court Bouillon around fish. Bring to a boil. Reduce heat to barely simmer. Cover and simmer for 3 minutes. Let fish cool in liquid for 10 minutes. Take fish from liquid. Cool. Peel off skin and remove bones carefully.

*Mushroom Duxelles:*

1/2 lb. very finely chopped mushrooms
1/3 cup butter
1/4 cup finely minced shallots
1/2 tsp. salt
1/4 tsp. white pepper

Put mushrooms in paper towel and press to get rid of excess moisture. Melt butter in skillet until hot and foamy. Add mushrooms and shallots and stir constantly until mushrooms look dry. Season well with salt and pepper. Cool.

## MON GRENIER'S SALMON IN PUFF PASTRY WITH BEARNAISE SAUCE (Continued)

*Quick Puff Pastry:*

1 1/2 cups flour
1/2 tsp. salt
3/4 cup (1 1/2 sticks) cold butter
2/3 cup ice water

Put flour in bowl and stir in salt. Cut butter into chips the size of almonds. Turn butter chips over in flour to coat them. With a fork, stir in just enough iced water so the mixture can be gathered together in a dough ball. (Knead just enough to get it together). Wrap in waxed paper and chill for at least 1/2 hour. Roll dough on floured board (or marble) into a rectangle about 8 x 20 inches long. Fold it in thirds and give it a quarter turn (folds will be at sides). Roll it into a rectangle, fold it and give it a quarter turn again. Add one more time for a total of 3 rollings and folding. Wrap dough and refrigerate overnight. Can be frozen, but thaw a day before it is to be used. **Do not** double recipe, make it twice.

*To assemble:*

Roll each dough ball out an inch wider than salmon steaks, about 7-8 inches and 20-22 inches long. Top each salmon with a large spoonful of mushrooms. Cut dough just long enough to be able to fold over. Brush edges with beaten egg and pinch together. Refrigerate as you're working. When ready to bake, brush tops with remaining egg. Bake in 425' oven for 20-25 minutes or until golden brown. Serve with Bearnaise Sauce.

*Bearnaise Sauce:*

1 cup butter
2 Tbsp. shallots
1 cup tarragon vinegar
2 Tbsp. dried tarragon
6 egg yolks
4 Tbsp. cold water
1/2 tsp. salt
1/4 tsp. white pepper

Melt butter and keep very hot. Put shallots, vinegar and tarragon in a small heavy pan and cook stirring with a wooden spoon, over moderately high heat until all liquid evaporates. Put egg yolks in blender. Add cold water, salt and pepper for 2 minutes. With a spatula, add tarragon mixture to blender. Turn on blender and add hot butter through top in a slow stream. Makes about 2 cups sauce. Keep warm in top of double boiler.

## CHILLED ZUCCHINI SOUP

4 cups peeled sliced zucchini
2 cups water
2 tsp. salt
1 medium onion, quartered
1 cup sour cream
2 Tbsp. vinegar
Salt, pepper and dill to taste
Minced chives

Cook zucchini in water along with salt and onion until zucchini is tender. Cool in liquid. Puree in food processor or blender a cupful at a time. With last cupful add sour cream to blend and add to zucchini puree in bowl. Add vinegar and blend. Season with salt, pepper and dill to taste. Refrigerate for a few hours before serving. Sprinkle with chives. Makes 8 servings.

*Grandma Dot never thought of this recipe as "nouvelle cuisine" but it tastes as rich and delicious as vichyssoise and doesn't have those calories.*

## POACHED PEARS WITH L'ERMITAGE CUSTARD SAUCE

8 whole pears
Lemon juice
3 cups water
2 cups sugar
1/2 cup butter
1 cup brown sugar
Freshly grated nutmeg
1/4 cup heavy cream
2 Tbsp. Grand Marnier

Peel pears, leaving stems intact and core from bottom. Sprinkle with lemon juice. Put water and sugar in a large saucepan over low heat. Heat until sugar dissolves. Bring to a slow boil, then reduce heat to simmer and cook for three minutes. Place pears, stems up in pan. Simmer, covered until pears are tender, about 20 to 25 minutes. Turn occasionally. Drain pears.

Melt butter in skillet. When it bubbles, add pears and brown sugar. Stir around pears until sugar is dissolved. Turn pears over and over. Add nutmeg. Continue basting, add cream and blend. Add liqueur. Serve with Custard Sauce.

*Custard Sauce:*

1 cup whipping cream
1 cup milk
4 egg yolks
1/2 cup sugar
1/2 tsp. vanilla

Combine cream and milk in top of double boiler and heat until scalded. Beat egg yolks until light and add sugar. Add to hot mixture and cook and stir over boiling water until mixture coats spoon. Stir in vanilla. Cool.

# Dessert Cart Favorites

THE BISTRO'S CHOCOLATE SOUFFLE

THE DESSERT FACTORY'S AMARETTO MOUSSE PIE

LA SERRE'S KIWI TART

AUX DELICES PARIS BREST

L'ERMITAGE CHOCOLATE GATEAU

## THE BISTRO'S CHOCOLATE SOUFFLE

6 - 8 oz. semi-sweet chocolate
3 tsp. powdered instant coffee
5 Tbsp. liqueur (orange, chocolate, almond, cherry or water)
1/2 cup flour
2 cups cold milk (or half and half)
1/2 tsp. vanilla
5 eggs, separated
2 egg whites
Pinch salt
1/2 cup sugar
Powdered sugar
Whipped cream, slightly sweetened

Butter a 2 qt. souffle dish and encircle with a buttered 2'' collar of foil. In top of double boiler, combine chocolate (broken into small pieces), instant coffee and liqueur (or water). Stir until mixture is smooth. Set aside to keep warm. Put flour into heavy saucepan. Slowly add cold milk, stirring with a whisk until smooth. Set pan over moderate heat and stir constantly until mixture is thick and smooth. Continue to stir for a minute and blend in melted chocolate and vanilla and remove from heat. Beat 5 egg yolks slightly; stir in a few tablespoons of chocolate and then back into chocolate mixture. Beat egg whites until frothy, add salt. Continue to beat until soft peaks form. Slowly beat in sugar until stiff peaks form. Stir 2 large spoonfuls of meringue into warm chocolate mixture to lighten. Fold in remaining meringue. At this point, souffle can be allowed to stand for one hour before baking. Bake in 400' oven 30 to 35 minutes. Sprinkle with powdered sugar and serve with whipped cream.

*From the moment the waiter spooned the whipped cream over our Chocolate Souffle, we knew we had to have this recipe . . . the girls in the class say that it's even better.*

## THE DESSERT FACTORY'S AMARETTO MOUSSE PIE

1 cup amaretti cookies, finely crushed
1/2 cup vanilla wafers, finely crushed
2 Tbsp. sugar
6 Tbsp. melted butter
1 envelope unflavored gelatin
1/4 cup water
4 egg yolks
1/3 cup sugar
2 cups half and half or milk
1/2 cup Amaretto liqueur
4 egg whites, stiffly beaten with
6 Tbsp. sugar
1 1/2 cups heavy, cream, whipped
Chocolate Almonds

Combine crumbs with sugar and butter. Press into buttered 10" spring form pan. Refrigerate until set. Combine gelatin and water in a sauce pan. Stir in egg yolks, sugar and cream. Stir over low heat until mixture thickens slightly and coats a metal spoon. Stir in Amaretto. Chill until mixture mounds. Fold in meringue. Fold in all but one cup of whipped cream. Spoon into prepared crumb crust and refrigerate until firm. Decorate with rosettes of whipped cream and chocolate almonds.

*Chocolate Almonds:*

Melt 2 oz. semi-sweet chocolate in top of double boiler. Stir until chocolate is melted. Dip bottom half of 18 whole blanched almonds into chocolate. Place on waxed paper. Chill until firm.

*A new feature on the dessert carts of many restaurants is now yours for the making.*

## LA SERRE'S KIWI TART

| | |
|---|---|
| 1/2 cup butter, softened | 1 egg |
| 2 Tbsp. shortening | 2 Tbsp. whipping cream |
| 1/4 cup sugar | 2 Kiwis, peeled |
| 1/4 tsp. salt | Currant jelly |
| 1 1/2 cups flour | Whipped cream |

Cream butter, shortening, sugar and salt together in electric mixer until light and fluffy. Stir egg and cream into butter mixture. Add flour and just blend, not beat. (Add a little cold water if dough is too stiff). Refrigerate for 1/2 hour if sticky. Shape dough by pressing into 10" flan pan. Prick crust with fork. Bake in 425' oven for 15 to 20 minutes or until golden brown. Brush with melted currant jelly. Cool. Slice kiwis and place in concentric circles around tart. Brush with melted currant jelly and refrigerate. Serve with sweetened whipped cream.

*It's good we guessed right on our first try at duplicating this recipe . . . we couldn't afford to go back.*

## AUX DELICES PARIS BREST

| | |
|---|---|
| 1 cup water | 4 eggs |
| 1/2 cup butter | 1 egg, slightly beaten |
| 1 tsp. vanilla | 1/2 cup sliced almonds |
| 1 cup flour | Sugar |

Bring water and butter to a rolling boil in a saucepan. Remove from heat; add vanilla. Stir in the flour all at once. Return to low heat and stir mixture vigorously until it leaves the sides of the pan and forms a ball (about 1 minute). Remove pan from heat. Put into mixing bowl. Beat in thoroughly 1 egg at a time. Spoon dough into pastry bag fitted with plain 1/2" tip. Lightly flour cookie sheet. Trace 8" circle on center of pan. Squeeze dough around circle closing ends. Squeeze another ring inside circle of dough just touching and another ring on top where the two bottom rings join. Brush entire top with beaten egg. Sprinkle with sliced almonds and sugar. Bake 1 hour in 400' oven until puffed and golden. Meanwhile make Praline Powder and Filling.

*Praline Powder:*

| | |
|---|---|
| 1/2 cup almonds | 1/2 cup water |
| 1/2 cup hazelnuts | 3/4 cup sugar |

Toast nuts for 10 minutes in 350' oven. Remove skins from hazelnuts by rubbing between a dish towel. Combine sugar and water in a saucepan or skillet, cook until light brown. Add nuts and continue to cook until caramel colored. Pour into pie tin and cool. Break into pieces and pulverize in food processor or blender.

## AUX DELICES PARIS BREST
### (Continued)

*Praline Filling:*

| | |
|---|---|
| 1/3 cup sugar | 4 egg whites, beaten stiff |
| 2 Tbsp. cornstarch | 1/2 Praline Powder |
| 1/4 tsp. salt | 1 cup whipping cream |
| 1 cup milk | 2 - 3 Tbsp. powdered sugar |
| 2 egg yolks | 1/2 tsp. vanilla |
| 1 Tbsp. butter | 1/2 Praline Powder |
| 1 tsp. vanilla | Powdered sugar |

Mix dry ingredients in saucepan. Stir in milk gradually. Bring to a boil over moderate heat, stirring constantly. Boil 1 minute. Stir some of hot mixture into egg yolks and then back into pan. Cook one minute more. Remove from heat. Blend in butter and vanilla. Cool. Fold in 1/2 of praline powder and egg whites. Cool completely. Beat whipping cream until stiff. Blend in sugar, vanilla and remaining praline powder.

*To assemble:*

Cut cream puff ring in half horizontally. Fill bottom with praline cream filling. Fill pastry bag with whipped cream and pipe over filling. Top with pastry ring and sprinkle with powdered sugar.

*One of the most requested recipes . . . after you make our version, you'll know why!*

## L'ERMITAGE CHOCOLATE GATEAU

4 extra large eggs
3/4 cup sugar
3/4 tsp. vanilla
6 Tbsp. unsweetened cocoa
1/3 cup toasted finely ground almonds
2 Tbsp. + 2 tsp. flour
1/2 cup sweet butter

Beat eggs, sugar and vanilla together at high speed of electric mixer until very light and fluffy, about 10 minutes. Combine cocoa, almonds and flour in sifter. Sift a little at a time over batter and fold in until dry ingredients are incorporated. Add butter a few tablespoons at a time, folding in gently. Pour into wax paper lined, well greased and floured 10" x 14" pan. Bake 20 to 25 minutes in a 350' oven or until cake tester comes out clean. Cool in pan 5 minutes. Loosen edges and turn out on rack. Remove waxed paper and cool.

*Chocolate Mousse Frosting:*

5 oz. semi-sweet chocolate
1 tsp. instant coffee powder
2 Tbsp. milk
2 eggs, separated
1/3 cup sugar
2 Tbsp. water
1/2 cup whipping cream
Chocolate curls
Powdered sugar

Soften chocolate with milk and coffee in top of double boiler. Remove from heat and stir some of mixture into beaten egg yolks. Return to chocolate and heat until mixture is thick and shiny, about two minutes. Remove from heat and pour into 2 qt. bowl. Combine sugar and water in small saucepan and heat to 232' F (soft ball) stage on candy thermometer. While syrup is heating, beat egg whites until soft peaks form. Slowly pour hot syrup into egg whites, beating constantly until stiff peaks are formed. Fold egg whites into chocolate mixture. Whip cream and fold into frosting. Chill overnight.

*To Assemble:*

This may be done day before serving; cut cake in two 5 x 14" strips. Put one strip on cake plate. Frost with a few tablespoons of frosting. Put on second strip and coat sides and top of cake with remaining frosting. Gently press chocolate curls onto frosting, top and sides. Place 1" strip of waxed paper down middle of cake. Dust entire cake with powdered sugar. Remove paper. Refrigerate until just before serving.

*"Thee" big dessert from thee "big" restaurant . . . for Thee!*

# Restaurant Index

## CHINESE



## FRENCH

## ITALIAN

## INTERNATIONAL

## MEXICAN

# Notes:

# Notes:

# Notes:

# Notes:

# Notes:

# Notes:

# Notes:

# Notes: